A WOMAN IN
A MAN'S WAR

A WOMAN IN
A MAN'S WAR

B.J. Olewiler

To order additional copies of this book, contact:
Xlibris Corporation
1-888-795-4274
www.Xlibris.com
Orders@Xlibris.com
20525

To my sister, Virginia Ann McPhee.

PROLOGUE

"Tacoma really is the jumping off place of the world, isn't it?" My mother's cousin, who had come to visit us from the East, made this casual comment in the middle of our living room to no one in particular. I didn't know what she meant exactly, but I did know when she was looking down her nose, although I could not have put it that way at the time.

Long before Seattle became the magnet that it is today, my parents decided the northwest was the place they wanted to live and they settled on Tacoma, a smaller version of its neighbor, Seattle, thirty miles to the south. This conversation took place not long after World War I when I was about four years old, so naturally I had no thoughts about WHERE I lived. It was just there. That phrase "the jumping off place," however, stuck with me forever and as I was growing up and understood what was meant, it seemed to me to hold an essential truth. We were out of the way. Things didn't happen here; they happened in the East and in Europe. We were always behind the times. It took a year for fashions of New York to get to us. True, Hollywood was beginning to make itself seen and heard, but then, California was always slightly ahead of us.

I see now that the relation between the east coast and the west coast somewhat echoed that between the old world and the new when the U.S. was young. At first, the new kid is seen as the uncultured primitive, lacking any sophistication; but then this upstart with no tradition to hinder it becomes the progressive liberal, one step ahead in many ways.

I only learned to appreciate the beauty that lured so many to the Northwest after I left there and the crowds had begun to erode the unspoiled atmosphere. Growing up, I accepted it as a normal state of affairs that one could get away from the city in twenty minutes or so to pristine lakes to fish undisturbed by others. If somebody else were there first you could always find another place nearby. And it was in the natural scheme of things to go crabbing in the Sound with a shovel, if you knew the right place where the water was shallow. Or build bonfires on the pebbly beach with impunity. Or drive to the ocean for the day to go geoduck hunting. What fun to find the new little hole they made in the sand and then try to beat these little creatures in their frantic dig to escape you.

My parents so often became enraptured with the sight of the mountain when it came out that I did know it was something special, and felt quite indignant that people from Seattle thought it should be called Mt. Rainier. Why, everybody knew that Tacoma was named after the mountain which the American Indians had named "Takhoma." Not the other way around. Thus, it should be Mt. Tacoma or Takhoma, if you preferred the Indian spelling.

Even if I had recognized the special beauty of my homeland, I believe I would have felt constrained by having to stay there. Perhaps it is the same restlessness that brought my maternal ancestors to the west after the Civil War which runs in my blood, or a certain curiosity about unfamiliar things and places, but I know that I was never one of those who say they could never leave their homeland.

Indeed, I was one of those children who never wanted to be left behind. No matter what the destination, I always wanted to go, too. So it came as quite a shock, when at the time of that visit from my mother's cousin, I learned from her daughter that there were times that I should be glad to be left behind. The two of us were playing dolls in the backyard there in Tacoma, and

Marvel, who was exactly two years older than I was (and behaved, I thought, as if she felt her name befitted her exactly) often baffled me with her remarks. Now she stopped and looked at me meaningfully, as if she had just made a great discovery.

"Aren't you glad you're not a boy?" she said.

"Why?" I said, nonplussed. Such an emotion was beyond my comprehension. I felt it was like asking me, "Aren't you glad the sky is blue and not green?"

She shook her sleek brown hair, "bobbed" in the same manner as her up-to-date mother's, and answered triumphantly.

"Well, you know only boys have to become soldiers and go to war. We won't have to do that. We'll never have to go to war."

"Oh," was all I could say. I hardly wanted to tell her that my favorite game was one my brother, Miles, and I called "Marching Off to War." Miles and I would fold old newspapers into triangular soldier hats, grab the large metal dishpan from the kitchen and beat it frantically, as we marched off to our imaginary war. Nor did I want to tell her that no matter what a war was I didn't want to be left behind. Until this conversation with Marvel, it had never occurred to me that I could not accompany my brother to a real war. Indeed perhaps this was the first inkling I had that there might be disadvantages in being a girl, a new and unsettling thought.

Of course, at this point I had no idea of what a war really was. Nor did a I spend my youth wishing for a war to march off to. In grade school, we children celebrated Armistice Day to commemorate the end of The World War, naturally accepting the comforting premise spooned up to us that we were celebrating "the war to end all wars" and make the world "safe for democracy." The fact that it was called "The World War" made it obvious that this was unlike all those other conflicts involving only a few countries. How surprised we would have been to know that before too long we would be called upon to add the number II after the name.

All of The World War books I devoured growing up had taught us there were no good wars. I suffered with the young

German soldier in Remarque's "All Quiet on the Western Front" as he puzzled about the meaning of war; and with Hemingway's romantic star-crossed couple in "A Farewell to Arms," who try to escape the horrors of war. Such novels purposely cultivated a deep conviction of the futility of all wars, which I subscribed to completely in my younger years. I was quite in accord with my contemporaries in feeling sure that war had been outlawed. Not in our enlightened era! But by the time I was a teenager this optimism had eroded somewhat. The talk of another world war arose quite frequently, and by the time I graduated from high school in 1933, the name Adolf Hitler was appearing in the news. Still, it was many years before there was any great alarm in this country. The tales that travelers brought back from Germany were about the remarkable efficiency of the trains and the building of the wonderful new Autobahn (the four lane superhighway) not about the darkness that was waiting to engulf us. For some time the leaders of the former Allies had tried one way or another to avoid another conflict like the first World War. And for the ordinary citizen there was little doubt that a way would be found.

In this atmosphere it was difficult to turn my back on the deeply felt anti-war sentiment, but in my teens, no doubt spurred on by my father's indignation, (he had volunteered for World War I, despite having two very young children at home) I gradually became thoroughly convinced that here was one case where war would be justified. First the Sudetenland fell to Hitler in 1936; then Austria and Czechoslovakia, and no one did anything. He was overrunning other countries. Obviously Germany was on its way to conquer the world and it seemed to me something had to be done about it. I wrote letters to the Editor deploring our isolationism. I said things like we had to stand up and be counted and that we were like the ostrich hiding its head in the sand. (Well, I was in my teens.) I spouted off whenever possible, but I was swimming against the current because this was far from the consensus at the time. The great majority of my contemporaries would vote "No" when asked if they would be willing to fight a war on foreign soil. The United States remained pacifistic, isolated, and neutral, with few dissidents.

Still, this was during the depth of the Depression, so I had little time to worry about anything else than fulfilling my strong desire to go to college. My brother, who was three years older than I, was enrolled at the University of Washington in Seattle and I yearned to join him. Sometimes it seemed touch and go. It was not uncommon during those years for girls to be denied access to college in favor of the boys in the family. I had good grades in high school, but such a thing as a scholarship never crossed my purview, if there were such things for girls, and jobs on the side for shy, inhibited teenagers were non-existent. I knew it would be a financial hardship for my parents with two children in the wings, even though the tuition per quarter at the University was less than today's price of a ticket to a Broadway show. In fact, I had to stay out of school one year after high school which kept me on edge, but in the back of my mind I knew that my mother would do her best to see that I was given the opportunity, even if my father might have thought it unnecessary. And then, I won the huge sum of $285.54, by tying for second in an "Old Gold" contest, (a great puzzle where you matched one of the names listed below to pictured scenes; for example, "Sandro Boticelli' matched the scene of a robot walking around two men playing cellos on a sandy beach. Wonder why those puzzles don't come back?) This tidy amount of money kept me going for some time.

When I finally graduated, I had a degree in Psychology which I had to accept was not one to impress prospective employers. During those years in school, I had often tried to get counseling from my my professors as to how to put my education to use, but these conversations all turned out the same way.

"Don't worry. You'll just get married," said one professor I remember in particular. He looked like a typical white-haired Einstein type and he smiled in a grandfatherly way, as if he'd given me a compliment. Then he folded up his papers and waited for me to go.

Even my favorite Philosophy professor, a much younger (and I thought more progressive) man I could talk to, said in a resigned way, "You know, you'll get married as soon as you finish college. Too bad to waste a mind, but your education may not be entirely wasted. It will stand you in good stead in raising a family, I suppose."

I wished that I had the temerity to jeopardize my grades by telling them what I though of their "guidance." At night with the blankets pulled securely around my neck as I dozed off in our dormitory room in the sorority house I would visualize myself the next time rising up and saying something like "You don't seem to understand, sir, that I do not see marriage as the only end for which I was born. I have other dreams besides a white cottage with a picket fence." But I could never work up the courage to take such a revolutionary step.

My parents were no better than my professors. Although they pretended interest and acted politely impressed when I brought home an "A," I could see they were much more impressed when I brought home a football player.

"A woman's main ambition in life has to be to find the right husband," my father said on many occasions, speaking with neither regret nor satisfaction, but with the assurance that comes from speaking matter-of-factly.

Of course, he knew very well this would make me angry, and we would get into one of the heated arguments that were frequent in our house, debates all of us relished (although I've no doubt that my sister would say there was one who relished it more than others). And though I know my father had my welfare in mind, he truly did think a woman's fate-ordained place was as a helpmate to her husband, even though my mother didn't altogether understand this. Assuredly he was not alone in this belief. The year after high school my then-boy-friend expressed the common sentiment. He told me that he would certainly not want his wife to work. That would mean she was taking a job away from a man who had to support a family. When I heard this I yearned more than ever for the chance to go to college.

Of course later "Rosie the Riveter," the poster girl to promote the woman working to help the war effort, brought a change of heart about women working that lasted through the war. However, when the war ended we discovered the acceptance and encouragement was not altogether permanent.

I was only four years old when the nineteenth amendment gave women the vote so I don't know how my father felt about that, but I would imagine he would not have told my mother if he had opposed it. As she told me many years later, on their honeymoon when Father demanded that she go for a walk with him when she didn't want to, she decided that this had to be the time to make sure she was not going to spend her life completely ruled by her husband's wishes as was the lot of her mother and grandmother. How she did this, I'm not sure, but in the everyday concerns or controversies in our family, she held the reins. I often wonder how different, with her strengths of conviction, she might have been had she lived in today's world.

One thing on which they both agreed was that I must get married, before the window of opportunity had passed. My mother, while she tried to pretend indifference to the notion that I was in danger of becoming an old maid, said on my twenty-third birthday, "I've always thought that was a nice age to get married. I was a little too young, I think." This last was an obvious sop to my pride, since she was almost twenty-two when she and my father married. After graduation, one after the other of my friends got married, and I watched, not with the envy you might expect from an insecure young girl of marriageable age in those days but with a definite feeling of something like escapism. Not that I was against marriage, but I kept thinking, "No. No. Not yet. Not me."

As the Depression languished on and on, and jobs in Psychology were nonexistent, I had to return to my home in Tacoma and look for a job, any job. I ended up in a place I dreaded: behind a typewriter, first at a loan company and then at an insurance company. As often as I could during the next two years I drove the thirty miles to Seattle to be with my college friends away from my uninspiring situation.

It was at this time in September 1939, after Hitler struck at Poland that finally France and England declared war on Germany. Even then, the feeling in America was mostly one of "let's not get involved in other people's wars." Those of us who felt we should participate were definitely in the minority; perhaps partly because little of note was happening in Europe. These were the years of the "phony war," when it seemed maybe the war would be stalemated forever, although the possibility of entering this war became always more conceivable.

That conversation that I had with my cousin, Marvel, about girls not having to go to war would come back to me now and then, when our involvement was no longer unthinkable. I still did not want to be left behind. My sister, whom we called Tines, and who was my greatest confidante, sometimes talked with me about the possibility of the U. S. getting involved and we tried to bring it down to our own lives. She, the more practical one, did not share my desire not to be left behind. She would look at me with that sisterly look of skepticism and complete knowing intimacy, folding her arms in front of her.

"But what would you do? You don't want to be a nurse." She would say flatly, shaking her striking strawberry blonde curls.

"No, But there must be something. Like driving ambulances, maybe." True, there was little place for women, except as a nurse, in any of those World War books. Still, the hero of "Farewell to Arms" had been an ambulance driver. Maybe they'd take women now. Somehow I managed to conjure up a picture of myself as a wraith in white giving comfort and solace to demoralized soldiers, nurse or no nurse. Little did I know how far removed this fantasy was from my actual incarnation as a donut girl overseas during World War II.

In the meantime, since there was no immediate prospect of war, I felt the need to "broaden my horizons", and "fulfill my potentialities" two of my over-used phrases of the moment. Seattle still seemed just a little larger "jumping off place" than Tacoma to my eyes, so I thought the answer would be a large, cosmopolitan city, where I would become a sophisticated cosmopolite just by living there. I teamed up with a sorority sister, Nancy, of like mind and in the fall of 1940 headed for San Francisco. We settled on San Francisco rather than New York or Chicago, mostly because it was closer and somewhat familiar, and then, too, it had all the exoticism associated with the Herb Caen's nickname for it—"Baghdad By the Bay." Nancy was an extreme optimist, reacting with exuberance to any slight bit of good fortune, pointedly licking an ice cream cone with the gusto of a child, which made it seem the smart thing to do, rather than unsophisticated.

And there was no doubt that we were becoming sophisticated. We perfected the feat of jumping on the cable car with the studied nonchalance of old-timers; on the weekends we walked in the fog to Fisherman's Wharf, delighting in the pots and pots of crabs; (we could pick out one of these delicious treats for fifteen cents!), and sometimes we took the train to Carmel-by-the-sea for an overnight if we could afford it. We, like everyone else in those days, worked Saturday mornings so it was a great rush to catch the train, but we thought it well worth it as we stretched out on the beach.

Naturally, friends from Seattle often looked us up, and we introduced them to babas au rhum and drinking scotch and sodas on the Top of The Mark overlooking the bay. Oh, yes. No doubt we were cosmopolites. We also sniffed at people who wore white shoes in the summer.

"Tourists," we'd scoff. "They probably call the city 'Frisco,' too."

Real city girls. That was us. We were there a little over one year, and we felt like Washington state transplants with jobs and all. I had even booked my passage on a trip to Hawaii, at a slight discount. Maybe the jobs were not the ones we'd dreamed of; certainly I didn't feel that I was "fulfilling my potentialities" but the Depression was not over and a job was a job. Mine was as a Teletype operator—not a very good one—for the Matson Navigation Company, which owned the main line of cruise ships to Hawaii and other Pacific islands. Over the Teletype, a very modern convenience, I communicated with the New York office to receive and confirm bookings. It was like talking on a telephone only by typewriter. Although anything to do with a typewriter seemed like dullsville to me, it was quite astonishing, at first, to type a question like "What date did you want?" and have the answer appear right back on your typewriter, "January 31, 1941," typed by somebody in New York. (Something like today's instant Email.) My astonishment did not take long, though, to disappear into the sea of boredom. We knew we were living in the modern world and we took it for granted that new inventions would come along, And yet at the same time we felt ourselves so modern that "things had gone about as far as they can go," like every generation before or since. It takes a long, long life to recognize this misconception. I often think looking at the thoroughly hip youngsters of today how surprised they'll be to discover some day that they are old-fashioned.

The west coast had become collectively nervous about being the nearest target to Japan, and everyone was volunteering for some kind of work to prepare for war. And because I could operate the Teletype, I could do my volunteer work on it, practicing to keep in touch with certain strategic places via this machine in case of the emergency. There were blackout dry runs, block captains and designated shelters. Although it remained an inconceivable something that we were preparing for, the arguments about the war in Europe became more and more strident. Of all my friends I seemed to be the only one who felt strongly that we had to do our part to stop what was happening in Europe, and in no way did that work to keep me diplomatic about voicing my opinion.

ONE

Nancy went to church that morning of December 7,1941, leaving me alone in our apartment. Sunday was cleaning day, and our tiny apartment presented some real challenges. Our belongings were crowded on top of each other so that cleaning meant we had to move everything twice. We had to move the sofa to get at the bookcase, and the little table in the kitchenette blocked the access to the counter top behind. This cleaning problem was only one of the several inconveniences that went with our home. If we wanted to use the oven, it was vital to remove the crackers and cereal we had stored there. Fortunately, the few times we forgot to do this, we remembered just in time to avoid a fire. We accepted all these inconveniences with youthful disregard. Or, to be quite truthful, we accepted them in order to say we lived on Nob Hill across from the Mark. To live on the top of Nob Hill across from the Hotel Mark Hopkins—how snazzy could you be? We never mentioned, unless absolutely necessary, that our little corner of this building was below the street level, nor that the building itself hardly lived up to its ritzy address. Tucked in between much taller buildings, ours had a plain brown brick facade, with unpretentious trimmings, plainly asking not to be noticed. Nor did we mention that the only light from outside trickled in from a small window in a window-well with an aperture so small we had to lean out backwards in order to see the sky and determine if we'd needed a raincoat.

On that Sunday I bided my time in my blue bathrobe, while Nancy prepared for church donning a navy blue felt hat, topped with a jaunty red feather atop the curls she achieved by putting her hair up in bobby pins every night without fail. (Permanents were not yet for everybody.) Many others put their hair up this way, but she did this without looking in a mirror, a feat that I thought extraordinary.

Left alone, I settled back happily at the table. Sunday morning breakfast was my favorite time of the week. I loved to while away the time, and, throwing all caloric caution to the winds, make myself a breakfast to make my mother beam: golden fried eggs, crisp (but not too crisp) bacon, jam-slathered toast. I turned on the radio filling the kitchen with Glenn Miller's music. True happiness! After a second cup of coffee and a delicious cigarette, I faced the reality of the vacuum, pausing to consider putting it off by getting dressed. I bravely headed for the appliance, but at that moment, an eerie silence broke the music, and then, in measured solemn tones came the announcement in a man's deep radio-cultivated voice.

"SPECIAL BULLETIN—REPEAT SPECIAL BULLETIN—PEARL HARBOR HAS BEEN BOMBED. THE JAPANESE HAVE ATTACKED THE AMERICAN SHIPS IN THE HAWAIIAN BASE AT PEARL HARBOR."

I hardly listened for the next minute. Must be a hoax! That was my first thought. Whoever was talking must be pulling a joke on us like Orson Welles' "War of the Worlds." And in such bad taste! Especially on the West Coast! Didn't they know we were all dreading a possible Japanese attack here?

But then President Roosevelt's very familiar voice replaced the impersonal one reiterating the message, and I knew, as did the entire country, that December 7, 1941 was no hoax and would be "the date that would go down in infamy."

I stood there immobilized with my hand on the vacuum, thoughts tumbling over each other in my head. The repeated announcements on the radio held no further fascination at the moment. Radio newsmen were not celebrities. They were merely disembodied voices deliberately coached to sound alike with no discernible accent whose aim was to prevent distracting us from the message. Yet, one had to digest the news. But how? There were no pictures to aid us, or to hold us spellbound. They came one at a time and days or weeks later in the newsreels. It was very difficult to imagine this disaster. All I could think of was the time a battleship (was it the Arizona?) pulled into the Tacoma Harbor when I was a child, and we were allowed to board it. I remembered how immense it was, how when my grandmother, leaning over the rail, resignedly watched her wrist watch fall into the sea—so far, far away. A ship like that—blown up? How could that be? In Hawaii? And I thought of all my friends who were just the age to fight this war, almost exactly one generation later after the first one. Now I realize that was a long time to live in such peace.

The disembodied voice from the radio carried not a whit of real communion. I had to have someone—anyone—to talk to. I went to the door but as I looked down at my old aqua chenille bathrobe, something stopped me. I heard my inner voice (read Mother's) saying, "You can't go out in the hall, looking like that."

I could do nothing but vacuum and wait for Nancy to hurry up and return. With great vigor, I ran the vacuum back and forth, back and forth, paying no attention to what I was doing. I hoped that Nancy had not stopped for an ice cream cone, her particular weakness, on her way home. I wanted to tell her the news.

When she opened the door, I leaped at her. "Nancy, have you heard?"

"What?" she said.

"They've bombed Pearl Harbor. We're going to war. War." I said, the words tumbling out of my mouth.

"War!! What's Pearl Harbor? Good Lord, B.J. What on earth are you talking about?"

"The Japanese bombed Pearl Harbor, in Hawaii." I said. "War, Nancy. We're going to war."

She looked at me, but no words came. For a long minute we stared at each other saying nothing.

Of course we never did clean our apartment that day. We called every person we knew in San Francisco and gathered with some to sit by the radio, not so much to glean further news as to share our feelings. The immediate transformation that came over the American population that day was apparent from the first moment and can be truly described as phenomenal. Now it did my heart no good at all to hear someone say, "Guess you were right, B.J.," but I can say with assurance that never since, in the many wars we have stumbled into has there been anything close to the feeling of unanimity and rectitude. Nor has there ever been the clear-cut justification. It was automatically assumed that we would be fighting the war on two fronts, and there was no doubt about what our path of conduct should be. There was only one route to be followed. This was now our war, and everyone must work at it. (There were some conscientious objectors, of course, who, unfortunately, were treated more like criminals than normal citizens.)

Years later, long after the ashes of World War II, when Nancy and I got together for a reunion, not surprisingly, we agreed that the thing we recalled most vividly of that unforgettable day was the exact shade of the old aqua chenille bathrobe I was wearing when I greeted her at the door.

I reported for work on Monday, December 8, not knowing what to expect. Still, it was quite a shock to walk into the vast building that housed the offices of the Navigation Company and find every floor commandeered by Navy personnel. They were directing the employees of each department to the appropriate place to acquire instructions, all done with a show of quiet efficiency and authority. Everyone not in uniform obeyed meekly with uneasy expectation. Somehow it seemed like an invasion of friendly liberators who, in that twenty-four hour span, had taken complete charge of our destiny. Of course there must have been some among us who were afraid of being liberated from their job, but I heard no vocal complaints. The booking department came together in a room, not where we usually worked, but where we could all stand as an audience. I looked at the uniform about to address us and was taken aback to recognize the face above it as "Jonesy," a former company booking agent. Apparently, he'd been in the Navy Reserve. Up until this day, he'd been a jovial kidder with no arrogance about him. He was as willing to kid with me as with the boss's secretary. Now, it was as if the uniform elevated him to a voice of authority and impressiveness, and we were already in a different world.

"Good morning," he said in a voice that sounded lower and more grave than I had ever heard it. "As you can see, the Navy has taken over the Matson Navigation Company. The ships will be needed for transporting the troops. I know all of you will understand the necessity for this, and that your services will no longer be needed."

After a few more words intended to be encouraging, he concluded, "You can pick up your paycheck at the desk at the back of the room by the doorway. Your bonus will be enclosed. Thank you for your understanding."

With my paycheck in hand, I returned to the apartment, only to find Nancy packing her bags.

"Fred and I want to get married before he goes overseas," she said. She had known Fred for six months or so and he was already in uniform so there was no doubt about his immediate future plans. (The draft had been in effect for about a year and he had been caught in its net early.) "And I'd better get back to Seattle anyway. I want to be with my family and . . . ."

I nodded in agreement. I knew now why I felt that relief at losing my job. I, too, wanted to be near my family.

It was very good to have Christmas at home that December of 1941. So many peoples' holidays were full of angst and goodbyes, that we considered ourselves lucky to have a normal celebration with no imminent farewells in sight. And once the holidays were over I was too involved in immediate future plans to give much thought to anything beyond. Tines had told me on her one trip to San Francisco to see me that she was seriously in love and was contemplating marriage. The war seemed to hurry decisions and events along, so shortly after Christmas I was preceding my sister down the aisle as maid-of-honor at her wedding. Since Tines is almost four years younger than I am there were some well-meaning remarks aimed my way asking when it was going to be my turn, but there was not a smidgen of envy in my happiness for her that day. We had always been close and I harbored a protective, almost maternal, feeling for her. That much difference in age of course can have different consequences, some good some bad, and as I discovered, not always correctly analyzed by the ones involved. Of course we had fights, usually about clothes borrowed or stolen, but I thought there was none of the usual jealousy and hard feelings associated with siblings. Instead of feeling that she was a nuisance to look after, as I might have, I preferred her company to almost anyone's and enjoyed having our little secrets. There are certain things only the two of you can share, especially grievances against your parents. That does make for bonding. She was my little sister. In later years I often bragged to my friends who did not know her, that we were exceptional in that we grew up with no sibling rivalry to speak of.

When both of us were past middle age and I said something about this perception to her, she said, "What do you mean? I would hardly say there was no sibling rivalry. Why I was always trying to compete with you, and of course you were always better. After all, you were much older. I know all about sibling rivalry."

That this view of hers came as a great shock to me only shows how mistaken one can be about the most meaningful relationships.

Not long after the wedding, my father was transferred from Tacoma to Seattle. I was glad to be back in Seattle—close to my college friends, the ones who were "town girls" when we were in college. All of them were married, most with husbands away overseas and their lives put on hold until they returned, so they had time for many an evening bridge game.

And before long, I found myself back at my dull typewriter

working for a large construction company. The Seattle office was in charge of a defense project at Excursion Inlet in Prudhoe Bay, Alaska. My brother, a civil engineer, was the manager on the site in Alaska, and later my new brother-in-law would be called to join him, so this job had a family feel to it. It had some other upsides, too, First was the pay—$42.50 a week, which seemed like a big jump from $90.00 a month. (The Depression was fast disappearing what with the many job openings because of the defense contracts and the disappearance of the main job seekers into the military.) Then, too, the extended family feeling in this company allowed my brother and me to devise, between ourselves, a code for messages between the two offices. The aim was to veil any informative dispatches from enemy eyes. Our code was not really sophisticated, and no doubt fairly easy to decipher, but when anyone brought me a coded message from Alaska to be transposed, I felt like an important part of the war effort. I loved the feeling.

But it wasn't enough. I still felt left behind. I wanted to be in the thick of things, near where the fighting was, so I began a quest to get overseas. Being a girl made this difficult. True, one could enlist in the WAACs (this was the Women's' Auxiliary Corps of the Army—changed into the WAC in July, 1943, skipping the auxiliary part}, the WAVES (Navy), or the Spars (Coast Guard) but when I looked into these different services, I discovered they could give no guarantee, in fact little possibility, of getting overseas. Further, if one did get sent overseas, it would no doubt be to a desk behind a typewriter—way behind the lines. That was not my idea of being in the thick of things. (Remember, It was not until 1978—thirty six years later—that women enlisted directly into the regular Army. Today I realize we will see no more men's wars as such. Women will be in there—maybe not fighting on the front line—but in there fighting.)

Then one day, coming back to the office from lunch, I picked up a copy of the Seattle Post Intelligencer, the local newspaper lying on the reception desk, and thumbed through it. A feature article caught my eye—an account from a female Red Cross worker somewhere overseas, exact location not specified. She described a life of ubiquitous dirt and hard work, serving coffee and donuts, coupled with a great reward—the feeling of bringing to grateful GI' s a "bit of home."

As I read this, I wanted to shout Eureka! My pounding heart said "This is it." I read it over and over again, repeating to myself the stated requirements: "college graduate over twenty-five years of age." I stumbled over myself getting to my typewriter, clacking out a letter asking for more information. Before long, a letter came back telling me how to apply, but after that came a grueling wait of a month or so. Finally, a notice arrived telling me that a field representative would be in Seattle to interview applicants on a certain date.

On that date I was up early trying to decide what to wear. My mother and sister settled the question for me, insisting on my navy blue suit and the little blue sailor hat with pink trimming under the brim.

"You look great," they said to my doubting eyes and so I hurried along.

It was a nice spring day, really warm for Seattle, and I had borrowed my mother's car for my appointment. (We were lucky to have two cars in the family in those days.) Almost a half-hour early I walked around the block of the Red Cross office building enjoying the displays of flowers and breathing in the clear, fresh air with deep breaths. Inside the reception room I sat down with two other girls obviously there for the same reason. We smiled at each other but said nothing. One of them looked very self-possessed, with her head held high, but the other one's constant fingering of the purse on her lap gave her away. When my name was finally called I was ushered into a room where a woman with gray hair coiled around her head arose and came towards me, holding out her hand.

"Sorry to keep you waiting. I had a few interruptions," she said in a deep voice with precise enunciation. No elision for her.

"Oh, that's all right," I said, looking up at her and reluctantly taking her hand, hoping she wouldn't notice the dampness.

She thumbed through my application while I sat silently smiling as brightly as I could.

"This is a nice recommendation from your former employer. What exactly was your position?" she asked.

"I was secretary to the vice-president of the Seattle office," I said,

"Well, yes. You know we are looking for girls who have a sense of independence and determination and well, sophistication. There is also the fact that it will take a lot of stamina. Tell me, have you done much traveling?"

"Not a lot. Just in the United States and Canada. We used to live in Chicago."

I didn't have to tell her that we moved to the West Coast when I was four, and I had only been back once, did I? And why did I let my family talk me into wearing this outfit which made me look about sixteen and about as sophisticated as a glass of milk?

She asked me a few more questions before standing up. As she shook my hand, she promised me that they would let me know. I thanked her, feeling like a wilted flower as I fumbled out the door.

Maybe the powers that be thought that at least I had determination when I wrote them another letter a week later after hearing nothing. In any event, after about a month, I was summoned to San Francisco for another interview. Fortunately, a friend drove me down and together we revisited some of my old haunts like the beloved "Fisherman's Wharf" and the "Top of the Mark." Perhaps it was this familiarity with the big city, combined with having someone to show it off to, that buoyed up my confidence. Maybe that's why the representative in the San Francisco office seemed so understanding, and reassuring. Ultimately, I was not too surprised, and more than delighted, when she welcomed me into the Red Cross. I was going overseas. Hallelujah. I was not going to be left behind.

In the days after I returned to Seattle, my family pampered me like a real heroine, since I was the only one of them going off to the war. My brother and brother-in-law had their jobs in Alaska and both were fathers of a new baby, so they were not eligible for the draft. My sister, Tines, the mother of one of these babies, had moved back home when Bill went off to Alaska, so was hardly thinking about joining any of the services. That left me to be feted. My mother made me roast lamb with creamed potatoes and peas and roast beef with my favorite Yorkshire pudding. On top of that the "sub-deb soufflé"—a chocolate mousse type of pudding served only on very special occasions—was put before me, as well as the blackberry roly-poly. I ate it all up with gusto.

Despite their understandable anxieties, my parents supported my decision. For the most part.

"You may be put in danger," said my father, hesitantly. "You know that?"

"Oh, no. Don't worry. We'll always be safely behind the lines," I said quoting the Red Cross line with confidence.

My mother hugged me, and said, "I'm proud of you, honey, and I'm glad you got what you have wanted for so long. But you know I think it would be so much nicer if you'd just found a nice young man to take care of you."

I'm afraid I just shook my head disgustedly. "Oh, Mother," I said. "You surely know that any nice young man would have to be taking care of me from the other side of some ocean because that's where he'd be."

The day before I left for Washington D.C., my friends held a bon voyage luncheon at the Olympic Hotel, complete with seafood cocktail brimming with our delicious little Olympia oysters. Of that group I don't believe anyone had been out of the country, except to Canada or Mexico. The Depression had kept us all close to home. Of course most of them had recently said goodbye to their husbands, but seeing one of their own sex off was an occasion. I think they were all very happy for me, and perhaps a little envious?

When I boarded the Northern Pacific for Washington D. C., I looked back to wave at my family with their tearful faces framed by the familiar peak of Mount Rainier out in all its glory that day. I choked back the sob filling my throat with the adrenalin and sense of adventure lurking behind it.

Composing myself I walked back to the club car with anticipation. I'm a great aficionado of trains. Back then, when trains were still luxurious, there was nothing to compare to their rushing spirit. You could move around freely, and especially on such a long journey—five days across the country—you were bound to become acquainted with fellow passengers. I feel it's a pity we have not seen fit to keep up our railroads the way they have in Europe. I keep hoping they will be revived.

I sat down next to a young man, slightly older than I was, who was wearing a Red Cross uniform. Of course I told him I would soon be wearing the same uniform and when I told him I would be going overseas, he expressed envy.

"I'm in Field Service," he said. "But they say I'm needed here more than over there."

He gave a little snort of disgust and disbelief, wrinkling his brow beneath hair touched with gray.

I didn't know what Field Service was, but he explained. It seemed to have something to do with logistics—getting supplies like scarves and sweaters to the troops, and getting help to GI's in need of counseling.

"Will you be going into Clubs or Clubmobile?" he asked.

"I have no idea," I said.

Other passengers in the car soon spontaneously joined in on our more general conversation. We all seemed to know each other at once. The common phenomenon of confiding in strangers on a train or bus (quite noticeably absent from plane travel) was highly augmented by the war wherever you were, but here it was intensified even more. We were going to be together for five days with little else to do but talk to each other, so talk we did. I heard confessions of sibling rivalry and problems with marriages and mothers-in-law and every kind of relationship. I got some things off my chest, too.

I remember one woman in particular who was going to Washington to see her boyfriend off. With tears in her eyes she looked at me rather beseechingly as she said. "I have never told anyone else this, but I really don't love him. I was going to break up with him two months ago, but he told me he was pulling out, and how much he loved me, so I just couldn't ditch him. I hope I'm doing the right thing."

There were two other young men going into the Red Cross, so they, plus Mr. Field Service and I made up a seemingly congenial group. I'm not sure how much we really had in common, though. The night before we arrived in Washington, when everyone was in a kind of sentimental, goodbye mood, the four of us were sitting together. Mr. Field Service, who had been with the Red Cross for some time and had impressed us with his importance, was confiding in us that the Red Cross was like any other organization. It wasn't what you knew but who. And he was able to pull strings.

"I mean it," he said to the men. "I can really help you a lot." Then he waved his hand at me. "Of course, this cute little doll won't need any help."

I sat there for another minute or so, silently fuming with indignation, turning over things I might say, my father's words about finding the right husband haunting me. I got up and stalked to another part of the Club Car. "Was I always going to run into the same thing—dismissal with a compliment? Hadn't anybody ever read Ibsen's "The Doll House?"

The next day, however, I had put my indignation to rest and when we pulled into Washington D.C. we all said goodbye with true sentiment, a kind of nostalgia for a time never to be repeated.

TWO

C oming out of the station, suddenly feeling very alone,
I hailed a cab. Pulling out the carefully hoarded paper,
I read off the address to the driver: Hurst Hall, American
University, Massachusetts and Nebraska Aves. NW. As we drove
through this wonderfully white city with its polished marble
buildings, and even as I got my first thrilling glimpse of the
Washington monument, threading its needle-like way up the sky,
I was aware of something amiss. At first I didn't know what it
was because I had never experienced it before and never expected
to. After all, hadn't I been away from home on my own for
several years? What I hadn't realized was I had always known at
least one other person well. Here in this great city, I knew no
one, not one person even slightly. I thought of the list of names
I had taken down with friendly instructions to say hello. The
idea of looking up a strange face made me shiver. Sternly I kept
telling myself there was nothing wrong but after a day of trying
to ignore it, I had to admit that impossible as it seemed, I was
suffering from a severe case of absolutely debilitating
homesickness. It snuck up on me when I wasn't looking and
threw me completely off balance. Of course I couldn't admit
what was wrong nor expect any sympathy. Neither did I feel I
deserved any. What had happened to the independent, undauntable
person I wanted to be? Somehow I couldn't find her.

My time for the next few weeks was spent in a group of two
hundred girls living in boarding houses or small hotels scattered

around the city. I was assigned to an old brownstone house with shuttered windows, four girls to a room. From there we gathered at the Red Cross Headquarters in the American University to get our instructions. Here we attended classes, listened to lectures about our duties overseas, and what was expected of us. We were even given quizzes on the material, but I passed them with little real understanding of what I was writing. We were also given many present chores of the moment, such as getting our pictures taken, trying on uniforms, taking shots, going through gas mask drills, and given a long list of items to be purchased.

As we followed these directions and went shopping for musette bags (something like backpacks) and cotton underwear for the tropics as opposed to the normal heavy rayon, it seemed to me that the one hundred and ninety nine other girls took it all in complete self-possession, while I just stumbled along after them, trying to keep my head above water but just barely. Then I noticed one girl who was obviously suffering from the same disease I was. I wasted no time in leeching onto her. I knew she could be my salvation. I asked her some simple question and she looked at me, glumly.

"Don't ask me," she said. "I'm completely lost."

"Are you homesick?" I asked.

"Yes," she said with anguished eyes. "Is it that apparent?"

"Probably only because I feel that way, myself," I lied.

Because she was in worse shape than I was, I knew that devoting myself to cheering her up would be good medicine for me and for a few days it worked. We clung together, as I kept reassuring her that everything would be all right shortly and she could look back and laugh at herself. This maneuver did make me feel better, but unfortunately did little for her. She was from Columbus, Ohio, and had not yet reached the required twenty-five years of age. Evidently an influential friend in the Red Cross had talked her into applying for this position anyway and she had done so without any great personal incentive. And that was the main trouble: it was not her original idea to go overseas in the first place.

"How can I build anyone's morale, when I feel like this?" she asked one day as we were waiting on a bench. She buried her face in her hands, looking up through her fingers for understanding.

"Don't you see, B. J.," she said. "I will never make it. I just want to go home."

After a few more days she gave up and left. I said goodbye to her, conceding that her decision was right for her. This was not the place for anyone who had been drafted, more or less. But of course I did not for one minute contemplate emulating her. I could never have faced myself, to say nothing of the ignominy I'd face, returning to friends and family after my role-playing as the heroine going off to the wars. My only path would have to be to struggle through without letting anyone know. I almost felt like I was back in high school again.

You see, in high school I had been something of a "drip" (today's "nerd" or "geek"). Getting good grades was just the first hurdle, which I was not willing to give up because of my actual interest in learning. Beside that, I was too shy to have the right social skills to be part of the "in" crowd and too proud to own to anything but indifference to being left out. Of course, I must admit when one of the really popular boys started showering me with attention, I spent a few months in a state of bliss, although I was careful to hide that fact from him. I suppose I thought I was protecting my independence. So when we had the final quarrel, he left me with the admonition that he should have known better than to take up with a bookworm. Naturally, my heart was broken, but I didn't let anyone know, not even my sister. I tried being a little "wild" for a while, doing things like smoking cigarettes and skipping classes, but that didn't go over too well with my parents, so I stopped skipping classes and smoked on the sly until they said I might as well smoke in front of them.

Fortunately, my years in college were much less of a disaster. It was not a complete disgrace to get good grades, and by joining a sorority I made real life-long friends who thought my fantasizing about something else than a dream-house and a dream-husband was merely a slight character warp. In my sophomore year when a great would-be pledge was blackballed only because she was part Jewish, I along with a few of my good friends, became incensed at the injustice, but could do nothing. Our sense of inequity was tempered by the comfort, security and sense of belonging that was offered by the sorority. This ambivalent feeling was one I have become very familiar with. Personally, I was becoming inured to the idea that I was always going to be caught between currents, allured by the ease and pleasure of swimming downstream with the crowd, but often finding a greater feeling of comfortable fit going with the upstream crowd. So I came to accept that my role in life was always going to be that of a slight misfit and that was all right— not quite with either the grinds or the butterflies but more accepting of both groups than members of either. With this insight, I felt that I had overcome most of these adolescent feelings of insecurity. I might be a late bloomer, but I saw maturity as just around the corner waiting for me.

But here I was now, in Washington D.C. long beyond adolescence, like any kid at a girl scout camp consumed with homesickness. I was thoroughly ashamed of myself, but I concentrated on concealing any signs of this weakness and pretending that I was drinking up all the new experiences I was having.

And there were plenty. Never had I been with so many people from all different parts of the country. The Northwest at that time was a pretty homogeneous place, populated mostly with people of Scandinavian descent or the Orient. When I was in high school in Tacoma, a major diversion for the whole school had been a girl who came from the South. Her accent was so exotic to us that it charmed all the boys and made the girls jealous. Then too, although the University of Washington was a large university at the time (10,000 or so) there were few people who were not from neighboring states or Alaska, (except the football players of course). Thus, this first contact amongst the group of Red Cross girls with different accents and ideas was dazzling.

The radio had to some extent homogenized the country at that time: the announcers all talked with the same accent, and we all had the same magazines sitting on coffee tables across the country. But the first few days in D.C. brought home to me that the sameness wasn't nearly as great as it might seem. There were girls from all parts of the country brought together here, and each one brought as part of her makeup, the different accents, idioms and point of view of her neighborhood. And there was indeed diversity. Little things like the astonishment I felt when a girl from the south yelled, "Wait on me." I had never heard anything but "Wait for me."

As soon as we finished training in Washington, several of us were sent to Camp Pickett: an Army camp for basic training in Virginia supposedly to give us a taste of what to expect. Our training was hardly stringent; actually a far cry from the reality to come. We were simply to mingle with the troops and help out at the canteen stationed there. Originally I felt my biggest hurdle was going to be that of throwing my early teachings to the wind in learning to accost soldiers even before they had a chance to whistle. However, after the first day or so this hurdle proved to be easily overcome. With surprising rapidity, we all gleefully threw off the "correct upbringing" that was part of our past. Our uniforms protected us from the charge of being "forward" or "fast" girls: they proclaimed for us that it was simply our job to be friendly and outgoing. It was a new fun experience to walk up to a group of men and say something like, "Hi, soldiers, how ya doing?" And then be greeted with surprise and polite delight. The Red Cross girls didn't often seriously discuss it, but we were in agreement that it was a new and welcome liberty. Had we been prodded, we might have said something like, "Hey, we can approach strange men without fear of being thought a "loose woman." How about that?"

Today's woman, who supposedly finds no difficulty in making the first move, might find it amusing to think that this could feel so liberating. On the other hand, despite the TV shows supposedly depicting life in the U.S., I dare say that many in the world we actually live in would understand quite fully how welcome such real freedom would be.

Although we were not to be entertainers, we spent a lot of time in that training period "entertaining" the troops in the lounges when they were off duty. There were a lucky few who could play the piano for group singing but most of us merely "hung out" or played cards with the GI's. One kind soul, seeing my lack of talent taught me to tell fortunes by reading cards. There were rather good-sized round tables around which groups could easily gather, so I spent a few hours telling this man he was going to meet a mysterious stranger or that man that there was going to be a new love in his life. I had just begun to get versed in this kind of card-reading when some of us were called back to Washington.

Pat, from Arkansas, and Arlene, a girl from Grosse Pointe, a suburb of Detroit, whose dark hair and blue eyes were a decided contrast to Pat's fair hair and brown eyes, were two of the ones recalled with me, and we became a sort of temporary trio trying to disguise our excitement. We knew we would be going on our way soon and wondered which ocean it would be. The answer came very shortly. We were to go to the St. George Hotel in Brooklyn. That meant it would be the Atlantic. A group of about one hundred girls including the three of us were sent off together.

The St. George was reported to be the largest hotel in the world at that time, and chosen so that we could get lost in the crowd; I found no reason to doubt it. It was a huge, massive hotel in a mostly residential area surrounded by the trees that really do grow in Brooklyn. We were told to stay in groups of only two or three to avoid revealing that we were a large contingent waiting to embark overseas. This secrecy was necessary to conceal from anyone with malicious intent who might be interested in the fact that a convoy of thirteen ships was to pull out of port at any time.

It was only too easy to get lost in this hotel and in the streets of Brooklyn and I was glad to have Pat and Arlene to lean on.

My naivete kept showing up in unsettling ways. Like that time we had to take the subway: I had never been on one before and I felt the depths of chagrin at dropping a coin on the floor instead of the slot while everyone in the group behind me had to wait.

In those last few days on this side of the ocean we went to the Brooklyn Navy yard to get our final gas mask training, our GI helmets and our little GI dog tags which we were to put around our necks and not take off until we got home or until someone else took it off. And on Christmas Eve of 1943, the three of us went to the church in New York made famous by Dr. Fosdick, which seemed appropriate on that family-oriented evening. We sat there quietly until I heard the one next to me sniffling, and soon all three of us had tears streaming down our faces without shame. Wasn't it our right, knowing that we would be leaving for somewhere across the Atlantic very soon?

On the very next day, Christmas of 1943, forty of us, looking very unlike a sharp military contingent, boarded our ship, the Samaria. Completely weighed down with musette bags and our heavy Red Cross shoulder bags, we were all peeking out from under our helmets trying to see what was to be our next mode of conveyance. The Samaria was large enough. It was an ocean liner that might have been luxurious in its former life, but now there was nothing remotely connoting luxury. The bare decks and railings were already covered with swarms of men in uniform, who all greeted us vociferously, but we were not allowed to stop. We were taken down below to a huge dormitory-like hold, empty except for bunker-bed iron cots to accommodate forty bodies. They may not have been very comfortable, but on this ship they represented real luxury. The thousands of GI's slept where they could find a spot—on the deck, on the stairs, wherever there was room to lie down.

During the day we girls automatically divvied ourselves up, and like the entertainers which we were not, did our thing. I particularly envied Arlene her ability to sketch a credible likeness of any GI and her foresight in bringing along the necessary charcoal and paper; her station had a long line waiting constantly. Under these conditions it passed for amusement if you could look cross-eyed, so blessing the person who had taught me to tell fortunes by cards while at Camp Pickett, I brought out my deck and set myself up in a circle of men. The circle kept getting larger and larger, and at first, I was very gratified, feeling that I was being really useful. My popularity, like any fortune teller's, lay in the fact that I'd spend a few concentrated minutes on the topic nearest and dearest to my listener: himself. I knew that from my experience at Camp Pickett, but I was unprepared for the complete credibility these men gave my predictions. Now that they were definitely on their way to an unknown future not of their choosing, anything took on added significance. Whenever the Ace of Spades appeared, everyone looked at the GI whose fortune was being read with real apprehension. He would not be coming home? He would try to laugh it off, mostly without much success.

After a while, I removed the Ace of Spades, but I had forgotten how many bad luck cards there were, especially the "other man" in a love triangle. I could see that these men, mostly not yet adults, had only one response available for facing something so unknowable: bravado and a good dose of "It won't happen to me," the natural instinct which makes it possible to go speeding down the highway. And yet for the first time in their young lives, they'd been called upon to give some consideration to the thought that it might happen to them, and my fortune telling only served to expose this carefully hidden emotion. So I gave up that game and tried a few games of poker, but I could never achieve the nonchalant attitude towards money that game required. I settled on pinochle.

Altogether there was an interval of almost three months from the time I hit Washington D. C. and my arrival in the United Kingdom. During this time we had been regimented along with the Army from one place to another, told when to move and when to stay. At this point with no coffee and donuts, we had nothing to work with but ourselves. It seemed, then, one had to indulge in noisy expressions of personality In order to build morale with such a large audience. Noisy expressions of individuality took many forms but whatever it was there had to be a little dose of exhibitionism thrown in. Few of us would have given Beatrice Lille much competition but we did become something like entertainers. And a small talent like the ability to touch one's nose with one's tongue could launch a person into celebrity status. We kidded each other about this tendency towards showmanship, but it wasn't all kidding. It came home to me on this trip for thirteen days with forty girls and thousands of men that I, for one, truly would not like to live in a world ruled by one's ability to perform, jealousy of another's popularity, or fear of being upstaged. In other words I would not like the life a celebrity. I came to the conclusion that It must be really boring to live in a world where self can never be laid aside. At bottom there is the trouble—self can never be laid aside.

Back then of course we did not have so many celebrities. The movie stars were the only ones that brought instant recognition. I had always said that I would not like that life of the movie star, with a sneaking suspicion of sour grapes, but with this experience on shipboard I saw I could say it with conviction. The constant competitive expression of individuality had worn me down until I would have welcomed anything with some objectivity. A nice debate about religion, politics, or euthanasia perhaps. Objectivity? Yes, in the way I am contemplating, because when you are really debating an idea, it is impossible to be thinking about yourself or your impression on the listener to any great extent. It is the idea that counts. You get outside of yourself.

Today it seems almost every young person is looking to be a celebrity on television. It's as if the only life worth living is the one to be celebrated on TV, no matter what the reason. And if that can't be attained at least you can live the life of others vicariously through the many magazines devoted to these "idols." And yet, it is often commented that strangely this privileged life turns out too often to have the concomitant of drugs and depression, accompanied by complaints about the lack of privacy. How come, it is asked, since it is the life that everyone yearns for?

The answer to that question is usually given in terms of "superficiality" without much clarification. But from this small dose on board ship, I saw what the trouble with the celebrity's life is—this inability to lay self aside. One must always be on stage with the focus on the "self" or personality. I think Marilyn Monroe showed her true depth when she was quoted as saying something like, "I could not live up to the expectations of the image I've made of myself." Never being able to lay this image aside became too much for her. I fear for many of the youngsters of today who may find their wishes granted. But then again, maybe there will be so many of these celebrities being instantly created that the overpopulation will have a therapeutic effect.

In spite of this slightly sour taste in my mouth, my spirits in other ways seemed to rise with each mile as we crossed the ocean. My prediction to the homesick girl was confirmed daily. My homesickness became more laughable the farther we got from home. My only intimidating experience came when I joined a long line waiting to get a final typhus, tetanus and typhoid shot. As I started to roll down my sleeve my stomach gave notice it objected to only two meals a day and delivered a knockout blow. When I came to in the sick bay, there were five GI's bending over me, as a grim-looking nurse arrived to find the cause of their concern. When the men told her what had happened her face went into a volcanic eruption.

"My God," she sputtered. "Here we have a sick man with a ruptured appendix over there and all of you waste your time on a sniveling girl who faints at the sight of a needle."

I arose and scurried out of there feeling I had betrayed my sex, but then I remembered the GI who, under similar circumstances, had fallen into the arms of a Colonel democratically standing behind him. That made me feel much better.

Our convoy took a zig-zag course across the Atlantic to avoid the U Boats or other such hazards, so one day we'd be headed north and then the next day turned to the south. This course gave us all something to do: to speculate on where we were going. We tried to work up excitement about heading for Africa when we zigged south, even though all of us really suspected that our destination was bound to be England, You could probably count on one finger the number of passengers on that ship who had ever been there, but London, in spite of the bombings we'd all heard about, was the least exciting of possible destinations, probably just because it was the most likely.

On the thirteenth day of this voyage of thirteen ships, we pulled into Liverpool, which was completely hidden behind fog. This cozy characteristic, so warmly home-like, endeared this city to me, although I could never vouch there was anything between the dock and the railroad station. I followed someone into the interior of a deep, dark truck, and the next thing I saw was an English train looking surprisingly just like the ones in the movies with its side doors wide open, waiting to carry us to London.

My first sight of New York had not been at all surprising because I had seen so many movies of it. Times Square, Fifth Avenue, the skyscrapers—they were just what I had expected. But somehow Big Ben, the Tower of London, Buckingham Palace—they had all passed by only on the pages of a history book for me. I had a feeling they were like myths in a story book never to be actually encountered, but here they were. It was as if the places which existed in a fairy tale suddenly came to life— quite a different experience from New York. Pat, Arlene, and I could hardly wait to throw down our belongings in the Red Cross boarding house and get out to see the town. We walked down the street, with no particular destination in mind, and ended up at Harrods, the great department store. We indulged in some inside window shopping—trying, without much luck, to find something exciting but still small enough to fit the limitations on our luggage. When we came outside we were surrounded by a suddenly thick fog making it difficult to see anything as we peered in the shop windows, so we were quite ready to stop at an inviting-looking tea house for the mandatory cup of tea. Three men in

English uniforms, who'd been sitting at a table close by, stopped on their way out.

"You are American?" asked the one who looked rather un-English with his dark, curly hair, and bronzed skin.

We nodded and told them it was our first day in London, and that we didn't know our way around. They didn't miss our obvious hints that Englishmen would be welcome companions.

"We'll be more than happy to show you our city," the tall one said. "And what a coup for us. We've really become disenchanted with American men taking all our English girls. you know."

"What do you mean?" Pat said wrinkling her brow above her large brown eyes.

"Oh, you haven't heard the old saying?—'What's wrong with the American GI? He's oversexed, overpaid, and over here?'— You see all the English girls fall for them without fail. They live on American movies, and all Americans sound like Gary Cooper to them. Besides they get paid a lot more than we do, so we English lads don't have a chance any more. Frustrating, isn't it? But now we have three American girls to ourselves. That's great, isn't it?" He finished with a gallant flourish.

As we saw it, it was our duty to engage in a little reciprocity, so we accepted eagerly, and we paired off as if prearranged. I got the one with the dark, curly hair whose name turned out to be Alec.

We really didn't do much sightseeing. That would come later in the daylight but for me, it was one of the stand-out evenings to remember. We took the tube and drank in the atmosphere of a foggy London evening. And then as the evening got darker and the fog heavier, we stopped in an English pub and I made the amazing discovery that Englishmen don't care for ice in their drinks. When we came out of this inn, the fog had become one of the famous pea soups, outdoing even my homeland's best. It had become hard to see anything beyond your reach. The six of us seemed very much alone; the blackout a real blackout. As any car would have to drive at a snail's pace there seemed little chance of one running you down, so we started walking down the middle of the street. Perhaps, the fog was so thick that Alec just figured we couldn't be seen but the first thing I knew this very polite, correct young man had me in his arms waltzing, actually waltzing, down the street while he bellowed out the strains of a Strauss waltz in a surprisingly strong voice. There was no denying his contagious enthusiasm, and the other couples started doing the same thing. Soon we were trying to outdo each other with great abandon. The waltz was the ideal dance for getting away with most any turn you felt like, unpracticed as we were. We danced on and on in the middle of the street until we were completely out of breath.

Like so many times that would follow with people I met overseas, saying good night to the Englishmen knowing we would never see each other again added to the intensity of the moment, bringing only a sense of adventure and no regrets.

THREE

T he next day in London we had our full force Red Cross meeting of this contingent that had crossed the sea together and I was very surprised to be given a choice of which branch of the Red Cross I wanted to join. Following instructions with no alternatives had become second nature, so it was with a feeling of slipping the proverbial leash that I raised my hand along with Arlene and Pat when "Clubmobile" was called, although I had little idea of what it involved. I was also surprised to discover that the different branches—Clubs, Hospital, Field Service and Clubmobile—operated completely independently of each other. Everyone who didn't go into Clubmobile left London immediately, and I saw few of them again.

Unsurprisingly, the name "Clubmobile" is meant to indicate a club on wheels, and these vehicles were unique to WW II and the ETO (and a few in North Africa early on). The Red Cross clubs scattered across the United Kingdom, where men could stop in for coffee and donuts, were only available to men on leave, so the Clubmobile was created to bring coffee and donuts to men on maneuvers with an eye to the forthcoming combat. While there in London, we got a peek at the ones being used in the United Kingdom. There were a few called Greyliners used only in England that might profess to be a club, with a space in the back where six or eight men could make a pretense at lounging, but the more numerous ones and the kind I was soon to be ensconced on was a more compact type, mounted on an English

Bedford chassis. These reminded me of a hamburger stand, with room only for a crew of three girls inside. They had an opening on the side with a serving counter to be let down. You entered by a small double door in the back that had a step to pull down and the inside was a narrow and rather awkward aisle with the donut machine in the place of honor. Everything else—the drawers and cupboards which held the donut trays, the portable phonograph, and the slots for records—were all made to be fastened down. Every time we moved, these had to be checked for security. (Forgetting to do this had unfortunate results. You needed only once to see the donuts, delivered out of the grease so zealously, lying mangled in a heap on the floor to become constant guardian of the locks.)

Eventually the same type of Clubmobile was mounted on the chassis of an American GMC 6x6-2 1/2 ton-truck, which were the ones we later took to the continent. At this later stage there were over eighty Clubmobiles that followed the Armies marching across Europe. And probably about half again that many remained there in England after D Day for the air pilots and other contingents still operating there.

Those of slated for the Clubmobiles spent the next ten days in London. First, we got fitted for trouser uniforms known as our "battle dress," which were necessary for the more rigorous life on a Clubmobile compared to the Clubs. These uniforms were so named because they were fashioned after the English soldiers' battle uniform. Naturally, the name always brought a hoot from any GI who heard us use it.

And then we learned to make donuts, our raison d'etre. As a child in Tacoma, I would often stop by the window in Hoyt's Donut Shop fascinated with the donuts, crisp and brown, flipping out of the machine every few minutes. It wasn't that I loved donuts so much; it was the machine that fascinated me. It assuredly never occurred to me that someday I would become on the familiar terms I was now thrown into. First we learned how to mix the prepared flour with the right amount of water. Then when we got it to the right consistency it was to be put in a pressurized can, which could blow up if not secured correctly. (Later in life, the new pressure cookers almost seemed like old friends.) The dough then was spewed automatically into the heated grease in the shape of a donut with its all-important hole in the middle. Around they went in a circle and at the right moment when they became just the right tinge of brown we fetched them out with skewers and arranged them in rows in the serving tray.

Learning to operate the donut machine was not really difficult: the hard part was getting inured to the overwhelming odor. Pat and I were learning together on the same machine and that first afternoon I said to her, "I think I may have to transfer to clubs. This odor is becoming really nauseating."

"Yeah, I know," she said, screwing up her perfectly shaped nose, "but I suppose we'll get used to it, eventually."

I was rather doubtful, but she was right. I suppose it's like working in a chocolate factory. The first enticing aroma must soon become deadly sweet, but after while it has to be unnoticeable. That was the way with us. Perhaps if we hadn't chewed on a few too many donuts that first day it would have been even easier, but it wasn't long before we were more or less immune to the assault on our olfactory sense. That is, if we didn't stay away from it too long. A week away and we had to get acclimated all over again.

After ten days of this indoctrination in the art of donut making we were considered skilled enough to cope with life on a Clubmobile, and were shoved out on our own. I was sorry to hear that Pat, Arlene, and I were to be sent on separate ways, but I was beginning to realize that life in the Red Cross was going to be full of such partings, and so we said goodbye, with very little breast beating and I never saw either of them again.

I received my orders and was surprised to find that I had been assigned to Northern Ireland. Surprised, because unexpected, but pleased at the prospect of seeing more of the British Isles. There were two other girls, Jo and Fran, also slated for Ireland, and we set out together, with our footlockers, bedrolls and musette bags to find Belfast. Jo had been my roommate in Washington

D. C. and though we had remained strangers at the time, it seemed good to see even a slightly familiar face and we were soon colleagues in our frustrating attempts to reach our destination.

From the beginning it seemed that anything would break down the minute we put foot on it. First a train in the middle of nowhere, and then after getting transferred to a bus, we had to turn around and come back to the station. After several hours of staring at the advertisements for Guiness plastered on the walls of the bus station, Jo suggested we try a little singing to combat the boredom. I knew this meant that she could carry a tune, so we started out with a little harmonizing of the barbershop variety, and went from that to singing some of the songs current at the time. When we got to "Sweet Sue," we began to feel right pleased with ourselves and each other. At least, Jo gave me a look of approval that I had never seen in D.C. An English nurse who had been in France joined us, and she knew all the words to "J'attendrai." It begins:"

"J'attendrai le nuit et la jour, (I'll wait night and day)

"J'attendrai toujour ton retour" (I'll wait forever for your return)

"Waiting for your return" was a naturally favorite refrain of the war and this was an especially poignant version, I thought. We had time to learn all the words before the bus was put back in working order and for me it will always remain the song of the war. When they told us the bus was ready, we looked at our watches, surprised at how much time had elapsed. I suppose that was the main reason that breaking out in song became a spontaneous American response to combating boredom and ended up building camaraderie throughout the war.

We were forced to spend the night in a little hotel in a small easily forgotten town and the next day we finally made it by nightfall to the port where our ferry would take us through the narrow passage across the sea, only to find that it had broken its rudder. And even before we had set foot on it! We sat up all night on its twin sister, which was to leave the next morning. Since we had had nothing to eat since breakfast, I began to think even a K ration would have been welcome, but there was no sign of food anywhere to be seen. (I suppose somebody had the bright idea of vending machines from a similar experience.) Sitting there through the long night in the cold breeze from the Irish sea, on a ferry that had seen better days, did nothing for our morale and we might have started snapping at each other, so we started laughing about it instead. At least we'll get our pick of the seats, we said. Fortunately, they served breakfast before leaving the dock.

The roughness of the Irish Sea deserves all its fame I must say. No exaggeration here. Even with breakfast inside of me, I began to feel that old queasy stomach almost as soon as we got started—an unwelcome reminder of the homesick days in D.C. Oh no, I thought. And here you felt so proud of not getting seasick on the ocean voyage. How ironic. Someone suggested going to the bow of the boat where you could catch the salt spray. I was thankful for the suggestion and spent the whole of the short voyage, letting the wind and spray wash over my face. I thought I had seen choppy water in Puget Sound, but the bow of this ship seemed to go down and up with an unmatched momentum. And the white caps were not just here and there, they were spread over the whole surface. At times the wind would lift a bit of foam from the sea and toss it around in the air as if it were a little bird. I was never more thankful to arrive on shore.

We took a train for Belfast which managed to make it without breaking anything, and there sitting at the station was a taxicab that brought the realization that we were indeed in a foreign country. The roof of this cab was covered with a huge balloon filled with natural gas, which made it look like it might take off in the air any minute but we got in and headed for the Grand Central Hotel. We were supposed to ask the Red Cross supervisor staying there for further instructions, but the clerk at the front desk told us that she had left for London the day before. As we stood there mystified as to our next move, with an attitude of helpfulness, the clerk told us there was a donut kitchen somewhere in Belfast that might help us out but he wasn't sure just where it was. So, thinking we could smell a donut factory we started walking down the streets of Belfast (whose name we soon learned to pronounce Bell-fahst with the accent on the second syllable.) By now, I felt quite sophisticated to be able to tell myself that Belfast seemed quite distinct from the English towns. It was the capital of the country and a bustling town but looked as if it belonged in the last century in some ways. There were horse-drawn wagons and streets of brick and what looked like clay or cobblestones. Altogether, a different Irish town.

We walked until we came across a small, rather ramshackle building, boasting an obvious new coat of white paint. Before we caught sight of the Red Cross sign, we knew by the casual stream of American uniformed men straggling in that it was one of our Clubs. The Red Cross girls running the club told us the donut kitchen was right around the corner, so we sailed around this corner and into the arms of a rotund red-cheeked little Irishman, who told us to call him Pop. He had a thick brogue, which we had to strain to understand.

"Ahhnd so, yoooure just oooover from the States. I spent many yearrrs of my life therrre. Would you like some coffee and donuts?"

We accepted his coffee, wondering how he had retained such a thick brogue and listened to his tales about his life in the U.S. He told us that he drove a cab in New York and loved fighting the traffic, but eventually the pull of Ireland called him back. He could not, however, help us in our dilemma of what to do, so we sat for several hours waiting for something to happen. The something that happened was a Red Cross girl who popped in to pick up some donuts. Somehow she knew that Jo and I were assigned to a base in Rosstrevor and Fran to another in Newcastle and even offered to take us there. Her familiarity with these strange names gave us confidence, so we put our fate in her competent hands and piled our luggage into a small English Hillman adorned with the Red Cross insignia, somehow managing to climb atop the pile. As we started down the road past the hedgerows and the thatched roof houses, excitement about being here in Ireland crept up on me. I felt very ready to leave the months of regimentation behind and start a new kind of life. I looked around at the Emerald Isle, drinking in its greenness even in the middle of winter, wondering how long I would be staying here.

Our guide turned out to be not so efficient in finding the places which had rolled so glibly off her tongue. After getting lost a few times, and stopping to ask directions of anyone in an American uniform, which were usually wrong, we finally succumbed to asking some natives and arrived in Newcastle at the Slieve-Donard where Fran was to stop.

The Slieve-Donard was a huge, remote building which in daylight turned out to be unbelievably ugly, but by night looked like a romantic castle, standing severe and impregnable, guarding its sweeping lawns. We could hardly achieve the sweeping entrance called for in our toy facsimile of a car, but we approached the entrance and Fran got out. Throwing her arms out dramatically, she exclaimed, "The moors. The moors. Heath cliff, where art thou?"

The three of us, new to this milieu, were more than ready to play along with her, so In favor of the mood I suppressed the urge to say that I thought "Wuthering Heights" took place in England. The scene seemed just right. The cold marble stairs and the long, empty corridor added to the impression and we silently crept around looking for something living. We could find nothing in this category until we headed for the dining room. There sitting at the other end of he room, dwarfed by the size and emptiness, was some red hair and a blue-grey uniform. We expected the hounds to come bounding out at any minute, but Fran sidled up to her and they achieved a seemingly silent conversation which was evidently satisfactory and we left her there moaning "Heathcliff. Heathcliff."

There was only one road between Newcastle and Rosstrevor, so we managed that twenty miles in less then an hour. It was very dark by now, so it was hard to tell much about the town except that it was on the inlet of water we had been following from

Newcastle. Our guide assured us that the Great Northern Hotel was a cozy little place, and she was right. There was even someone at the desk at this late hour who told us in a sleepy voice, "Ah, Aye, Miss Jane did say soomthin' about ye might be a coomin' in."

We ran upstairs and lovingly touched our bed, a luscious thing with a huge down comforter which put my grandmother's to shame. We could hardly believe our luck. We wouldn't have to sleep on cots! There was a bathroom at the end of the hall, which was a mite cleaner than we had been led to expect, and after perfunctory face-washing, I crept under the great comforter with surprising gratitude. I was ready for whatever was to come with happy anticipation. As I thought of my bed at home, it was not with longing, only with a warm feeling of knowing that in that house they were probably thinking of me, too. With a slight smile, I recalled my recent homesickness. It seemed like something that happened a long time ago to someone else more vulnerable than the person about to fall asleep. I snuggled into the comforter, happy to be there, looking forward to the morrow and whatever would come. I had not been left behind.

FOUR

The next morning before we had gotten out of bed we were greeted by our new captain, Jane, who came in to look us over. The one in charge of each Clubmobile was called a captain, but there was no real connotation of rank as in the Army's use of the word. Somebody just had to be in charge. Jane drew up a chair and sat down with a quiet, competent air which I came to admire greatly, and looked over her new crew. She spoke in a calm, accepting tone of voice.

"Welcome at last," she said, her smile placid but reassuring. "We expected you three days ago, but that's life in the ETO." I felt quite blase at being familiar with this acronym for European Theater of Operations.

"First things first," she said. "I think you probably need the day off to get your bearings and get yourself unpacked. There are just two of us at the moment, but we've been doing it for some time, and until tomorrow, when she leaves, we can get along without you."

She explained a few more details about the life in the ETO such as where we were to eat, how to keep track of our pay in pounds and shillings, and then departed leaving us on our own.

Jo and I unpacked our bed rolls and footlockers, laughing at the huge United States maps that we'd planned to hang on the walls of our clubs, the flower seed originally intended to brighten some African oasis and the cotton lingerie meant to withstand the humid Asian climate. We put our helmets, musette bags and bedrolls aside. knowing we would need them later but not now. We were still uncertain about the extra shoe leather and the hot water bottle—the kind filled with sand and a chemical that reacted to a tablespoonful of water—so we left these in the bottom of our footlockers to rattle around or leak sand for the rest of our sojourn.

Once unpacked, we stepped outside to see what Rosstrevor looked like. We had already learned that this was where the song, "The Mountains of Mourne Sweep Down to the Sea" was written, (although to my biased eye the mountains looked more like foothills), and made a stab at learning some of the words. We also formed a strong opinion of the Irish people's relationship with England from this popular song, which says in part:

"And they come across and try to teach us their way
And blame us too, for being what we are
But you might as well go try to catch a moonbeam
Or to light a penny candle from a star"

It speaks for itself quite expressively.

The road we'd taken the night before leading from Newcastle to Rosstrevor left the Irish Sea at Kilkeel and turned inland, following the outline, more or less, of a body of water the Irish called Lough Carlingford. The name "Lough" surprised me because it was mostly an inlet of salt water from the sea, and even sported a weak tide, which I don't think lakes are supposed to do. Looking across this lough to the other side you could, if you had a pair of binoculars, see the Irish Free State which was off limits to all Americans, because of its neutrality. So even though we could see it, Southern Ireland remained unexplored for us.

In describing Rosstrevor, the travel books are unanimous that it is a "little watering place nestling among the mountains." I wasn't sure just what a "watering place" was, but it obviously didn't mean a swimming place. At least I never saw anyone go in the water even when it became warm weather. But it did nestle into the hills. The road in front of our hotel was the main road through the village; It skirted the Lough on one side, and the whole town lay on the other side, climbing up the hills.

Across the street from the hotel, the embankment bumped into a long, low building situated on a little promontory. Jane had told us this was the kitchen and mess hall of Company I of the Fifth Division of the Army, whose barracks were on our side of the road, next to the hotel. At the moment I had little conception of how important this Company I would become for me, and I had no idea how many men a company would entail, but I was soon to find out.

Jo and I sat on a bench conveniently situated on the lawn of the Great Northern and watched several squads marching up and down the road. One after the other came by—a small group of men following the bellowed orders of the drill sergeant., "Hut, two, three four. Hut, two, three, four." All marching in step, they stopped, about faced, and all, with obvious signs that they had done it all over and over again and would expect to do it soon again.

We started laying bets on whether they would take ten in front of the hotel, attempting to foretell this by reading the character of the sergeant. Either he looked straight ahead and was all business, or with a smile he gave the order, "At Ease." We were delighted when so many of them did take ten, because our guide the night before had told us that the men we'd be serving were hardened veterans of years in Iceland and were bored to death and very bitter about their lot. As rookies in the Red Cross, we'd dealt with nothing but new recruits up to that point so felt great relief at realizing these young men might be veterans of a year or so in Iceland, but were no different from the ones we'd been serving.

I quickly took advantage of the situation to overcome some of my abysmal ignorance about the nomenclature and makeup of the Army. When Jane had talked about serving two companies or a battalion, I nodded sagely, but I had no idea whether she was talking about one hundred, or one thousand men and whether a company was part of a battalion or vice versa. I did recognize that the small segment marching by was a squad, because Jo told me so, but beyond that, the only clue I had was the notion of a regiment as a very large group, because my mother had always used the phrase, "Why, that's enough for a regiment" when I went overboard on a pot of rice or macaroni.

Assuming any GI would be glad to educate me, I cornered one of the first who came over to check out the Red Cross girls sitting on the bench. While he dictated, I took notes on a piece of paper, outlining the structure of the Army, including number of men, from the squad up: platoon, company, battalion, regiment., division, corps, Army. On paper, it seemed really simple, and made us both feel really pleased with ourselves.

That first night, Jane, evidently feeling that we should have our bearings in place by now, informed us that Company I was having a beer party in the mess hall across the street. We were all invited. Sneaking a look at my notes, I calculated that there would be approximately one hundred eighty men present. A beer party with one hundred eighty men and four girls! It all sounded rather fantastic, but if this was part of fulfilling my potentialities as a Red Cross girl, I was ready.

Dressed in our skirt uniforms, wrinkly rayons, (the wonderful new nylon stockings were now strictly unavailable as the nylon was being saved for the parachutes of the Air Corps) and the forbidden high heels that every girl had tucked in her luggage somehow, we started across the road, I with rather hesitant steps. Stag parties were not part of my repertoire, and I half expected to see one hundred eighty unruly men floating around in a sea of beer. The picture I bore in mind was, shall I say, unsettling? Like a New Year's Eve party where one ran a gauntlet of pawing hands. But I needn't have worried. When we walked into the mess hall, the men were all seated on benches at the long bare tables, quite circumspectly looking at empty canteen cups. They'd whisked down their throats the two or three kegs of beer that was their allotment long before we got there. Apparently it was just barely enough alcohol to raise their spirits. A boy named Ernie stood on one of the long tables singing a song with vehement expression, gesturing humorously with a long, black cigar. The song, whose every verse ended in "like a good girl should," was later cleaned up a bit for the "Hit Parade", but even then it could only be considered slightly risqué. Everyone laughed heartily at the right places, and I learned from the man sitting next to me that they'd witnessed the same routine at least monthly since they'd been together, which he appeared to think was somewhere in the vicinity of eternity, After a few more numbers by a guitar player, someone got up and suggested that the new Red Cross girls do a number. Jo and I looked at each other doubtfully.

"Go ahead," Jane said. "They'll like it, whatever you do."

"Well, we've done some harmonizing together," I said. "Shall we try again?" In this casual and friendly atmosphere, we felt there was nothing to be lost, so we picked "Sweet Sue" as an easy one and got up on one of the benches and started singing. As we did, the atmosphere turned from an easy and jovial nonchalance into an expectant stillness. Overtly the men paid had us little heed when we slipped into the party, but now every eye was riveted upon us. There was nothing nonchalant about the minute scrutiny they gave us. Every chord wavered, forlorn and lonesome, in the room so suddenly devoid of the friendly scraping shoe or tapping finger. Hoping to cover up our lack of polish and the awful stillness, I started keeping time furiously with one foot. Just as I felt the hissing should start, a GI leaned over and tapped me on the leg.

"Wassamatter? Yah nervous? Don't be."

I collapsed into laughter, suddenly realizing that this intent appraisal was not directed at our singing. We were being appraised on a different score—one made up of the customary man-appraising-horse attitude and the fact that all of our ancestors had once decided to come to the United States to live. That meant we were not judged on the same scale as the Irish girls. We represented the girl back home. After that, it was all right, and we led some group singing for a while and learned to know the names of a few of the men.

At the time when I had been envisioning this life which was now reality, I daydreamed about being part of a group, sort of a human mascot who looked upon the men as human beings out of the context of their uniforms. This daydream was never fully realized, but the closest I came to it was with Company I of the Fifth Division. Any of them left alive today would probably not remember me, but I developed a really chauvinistic attitude towards the division. It became **my** division although we only served one-half of it.

I don't know why, but I was allowed to stay there in Rosstrevor with Jane for over five months while other girls came and went. I was thankful because it meant that I became real friends with many of the men, especially the kitchen crew.

In theory, we were supposed to drive our Clubmobile to an outfit early in the morning, attach our donut machine to the electrical outlet magically awaiting us, and spend the morning making donuts. Then in the afternoon after the men's appetites had been whipped up by the luscious aroma, serve them the coffee and donuts. I understand this system was worked out with some success in parts of England around the airfields. But there was no way we could have worked it out.

The number of men was the first obstacle and a formidable one it was Our assignment, half of the Fifth division, meant somewhere in the neighborhood of eight thousand men. We had two regiments and the Field Artillery. My mother was quite right in her assessment of a regiment—it does denote an overwhelming number of mouths. The second obstacle, had we tried to follow the theoretical procedure, was that the outlet supposedly awaiting us where we served would always be at least five hundred yards from where we could park. To overcome these problems Jane, with the help of some of the men, had rigged up an extension cord from Company I's electric outlet so we could do all our donut making at their back door, where fortuitously there was just enough room for us to park off the main road. In order to make enough donuts for the day, a little Irishman, who looked a bit like the "little people" he said he believed in, was hired to work through most of the night on our Clubmobile and then we took over the next morning working until noon when we took off to the outfit slated for the day. That's how we became so cozy with the kitchen crew. We were at their back door every morning, except Sunday, all morning.

If we missed breakfast, which we often did because of the ungodly hour, there was always a pot of coffee saved for us, and we toasted hunks of thick bread on top of the huge coal stove, listening to the morning ritual of jokes cracked at our expense. The kitchen crew always acted as if eight o'clock were the middle of the day and kidded us about the wings we were earning for the numbers of hours spent in the sack.

After this we went to our truck, turned on the donut machine and waited for it to warm up. As we became more and more acquainted with the donut machine, we all developed a real animosity towards it. The grease gurgling around inside that ill-natured contraption was kept at 425 degrees Fahrenheit. Now, anything else allowed to fan itself up to 425 degrees, surely should have willingly parted with a little of that heat, but not the donut machine. The only thing it gave off was smoke in big, billowing clouds. Valiantly, the bantam flue tried to cope, but all in vain. We were always forced to keep the back door open because of the smoke, which made it very cold indeed, in spite of our long johns and battle dress.

As a matter of fact, we probably would have kept the back door open, fumes or not, as an indication that we were willing to receive callers. Without our callers the mornings might have been rather dull, but as it was there was always someone to brighten our day and parenthetically chew on our donuts. We became very chummy with some of the regular drivers whose job it was to deliver materials or papers between their bases and HQ; we were something like Eleanor's Hamburger Stand on the regular route of the truck drivers back home.

And there was always Company I. Depending upon which shift was on duty, we had the off-duty kitchen crew as regular customers and some incidentals who could spare the time. We had some fascinating conversations over the donut dough.

There was one regular, not on the kitchen crew: a big, well-liked sergeant from Hamtramck, a suburb of Detroit. (Strange, the names Hamtramck and Reykjavik, the capital of Iceland, both of which I had never seen and had to learn to spell, soon became familiar names for me). Bud, who always made himself comfortable wherever he was, guessing rightly that I had led a secluded life, set himself out to "sharpen" me up, contending that girls like me didn't know what the score was, which was a sad state of affairs. Draping himself on the counter while I forked the donuts from the dripping grease, he would set about "sharpening me up" at great length, having chosen me because I was the one who'd play along.

"Yeah, ya gotta get smart," he would say. "The trouble with you is ya don't realize everything is a racket. Ya gotta have a racket to get along in this world. Why look, ya never even heard of the numbers game." He'd wave his arms around and smile broadly as if he were dispensing a gift.

"My father got along pretty well, and he didn't have a racket," I would counter.

"Oh, your fadder. Don't give me dat stuff. Ya don't know what he does all day long. If he's smart, he's got a racket. If he isn't,—well. That's the trouble with your women. Ya gotta get smart. Take this Red Cross racket. I suppose you think it's on the up and up," he'd say, shaking his head sadly, with his wide sardonic smile," but it ain't. A legal steal, that's what it is." as he wolfed down another free donut.

I felt that I must've been wrapped in cotton batting and stored away in a cool, dry place for a good part of my life experience. Here was a whole new world that I knew nothing about. My "correct upbringing" sometimes seemed more of a hindrance than an asset. I thought back to the summer when I was a freshman in college and begged my parents to let me get a job as a waitress in Yellowstone Park. They were definitely opposed. It was not the thing to do. A young girl had to be very careful. The lesson we girls were supposed to learn back then was, in great part, to live with fear, fear of something around the corner waiting to harm us. We still too often, thought of ourselves as the damsel waiting for the prince on a white charger, to bring her happiness. I realized this, and had found it frustrating with no escape. Up until now, I had only watched as boys went off to a life of adventure. The strange thing is that today, with their much greater freedom there is probably much more reason for a young woman to be afraid of what might be waiting for her, like rape, drugs, or AIDS than there was in those days. We were certainly living in a safer era, but not because we were protected from the world.

Now in my new life as a donut girl I was constantly banging up against every-day circumstances that had completely foreign seams linking them together. Certainly my past-life experiences were not to be trusted. I felt this way emotionally, intellectually and in every day simple things like mixing coffee and cream. Having mixed these two substances together in my coffee with what I thought was all the possible permutations, I felt that here, at least, I was on pretty safe ground. But of course I wasn't. And Tommy, a first cook and our primary teacher of the practical side of life, knew it. His method of sharpening up was different from Bud's, though. He didn't tell us the answers first—that would be too simple. He believed in the trial and error method and had the patience to see it through. For instance, instead of stopping me, Tommy just watched the first time I nonchalantly dumped a can of condensed milk into the coffee I had just prepared in the vat, so huge it could have held a small-boned man as a cannibal's cauldron. Since it was he who'd heated the water for us and would have to do it again, I found his patient smile of wry expectation rather confounding when the whole thing turned into a curdled, horrible looking mess.

"The milk must be sour," I said hopefully.

"Taste it," said Tommy.

It was sweet, naturally, so I waited dutifully for the sharpening. It came as he poured that cauldron down the drain in the middle of the floor.

"When it's this hot, it'll do it every time," he said. "You either have to put some cold water in first or stir it with a big metal spoon to conduct the heat away.

I regretted the wasted coffee and wondered how much more of my training with dainty teacups would have to go down the drain. "But after all," I would say to myself, "who would dream that this day would come when serving coffee entails seventy gallon vats and cleavers as can openers.

Those cleavers were always hung up in an imposing row over the long worktable, ranging from a huge one about right for felling an ox, to one we used for our milk cans, which was as dainty as cleavers can get. I watched as the cooks using these cleavers gave deft, swift strokes to the cans, and when I thought I had the hang of it, I lined up my milk cans on the operating table and proceeded to do what I'd studied. I thought I was jerking my left hand away just in time as I had seen the cooks do it, but my "just in time" was too late and the can turned over on its side as I reached it with the cleaver, splitting neatly in two, spewing all the milk on the floor.

After Tommy gave me the lesson he knew I would need, I became quite proficient at cleaving open the cans. In fact, I often became so engrossed in the thrill of finding my left hand whole after each blow that sometimes I opened so many we had to trade opened cans for unopened ones with the kitchen crew. Having grown quite enamored of those cleavers, I missed them after we'd left Ireland.

Jane and I were often alone during those months, as a third

girl came and went and for once I counted myself very lucky to
be left behind. Jane was an accountant from Buffalo,. New York
so obviously had the kind of personality that makes it possible
to look at rows of black figures without distress. I often tossed
off the phrase, "She's a solid character," when talking about Jane.
I think it meant that she was comforting to have around because
she gave the feeling that nothing would go wrong. And there was
plenty that could go wrong. The trials and tribulations that rained
on the heads of the Clubmobilers were frequently and
humorously written up in a little paper called "The Sinker" which
was "published" (i.e. mimeographed) in London by the
Clubmobile department. For example, the donut machine would
break down at a crucial moment, a GI would be called in to fix
it, and his tinkering would cause the pressure can to blow up
leaving bits of dough plastered from ceiling to floor. Or a girl
would open the wrong faucet resulting in hot grease cascading
onto the floor burning both the linoleum and the legs of the
long-suffering writer. Naturally, I assumed this all was exaggerated
for the sake of wit, but later on I would find it was not all
exaggeration. At times during those months we were forced to
visit other bases in the vicinity to get supplies or give a hand in
the event of sickness. Then it was I discovered that such debacles
as described in the "Sinker" actually happened. The amazing thing
to me was the only thing left intact was the indestructible sense
of humor. That not only survived, it seemed to thrive on such
fare.

Then I would turn to Jane admiration dripping off me. I
knew if we had such days of things going berserk, my sense of
humor might not thrive so well, and I would hate myself for
being a poor sport, but Jane, the pillar, saved me from such a
fate, and I would sing all the way home, loving life, loving order,
and loving accountants.

Jane's physical strength was for a woman something special,
too. She outdid me in believing in the virtue of self-reliance and
disdained help with most of the physical shoving, pushing
and carrying, except for the two hundred pound bags of flour.

I, too, rather welcomed the chance to belie my apparent fragility by doing most of my own shoving and pushing. I had earned several nicknames like "Baby face" and "Tiny" and some that were bits of sarcasm like "Fatso" and "Muscles." So I thought I had something to prove, I guess. I did feel some sympathy for the girl written up in "The Sinker," who, after heaving several full coffee urns around, turned and said to the man next to her, "Oh, Sergeant, marry me quick, before I become neuter," but I could feel none for the girls who felt that the quickest way to a man's heart was to appeal to his big strong manliness. Opening your car door and lighting your cigarette may make him feel protective, but take it from me, scrubbing your floor and carrying your coffee urns only makes him feel tired.

This was especially true in our little corner of the world in Ireland, because all our heaviest work was done in the same place. When the theoretical procedure of baking donuts at a different base each day was actually carried out—as we would discover when we hit the Continent—it was not so hard on a man's disposition to be asked for assistance occasionally. But with us in Rosstrevor, installed as we were as a permanent appendage to Company I's kitchen, it was always Tommy or Mike or Connie or Frenchie who was the fall guy. Considering that standing over a hot stove all day is notoriously rough on the disposition, that they helped us at all was a source of amazement. Naturally there was one member of the kitchen crew who let it be known, not diplomatically, that he thought of us as nothing but a hindrance and a nuisance, so we stayed out of his way. All the rest of the crew rather ignored him, too, and obviously didn't agree with him. And all of us highly valued being accepted as a part of the gang back at Company I.

To cement our position, we ate most of our meals with them, although we could have relaxed over a white tablecloth at the hotel. I must admit this was not as great a sacrifice as it might seem. To be sure, we could get eggs with shells on them twice a week, which was a great treat. But that was about the only thing that was really appealing. Although I pride myself upon my tolerance for the unfamiliar, the unfamiliar morning sausage at the hotel turned out to seem all too familiar—like sawdust. The eternal fowl (though which fowl was never mentioned) always seemed to have pin feathers that tickled your throat on the way down. Trifles can be as tasty as they look, and the trifle in the hotel was always a lovely multi-colored creation, but somehow on its way down, I felt I might as well have eaten the centerpiece for dessert. I'm sure the Irish did their best with what they had, for they were quite evidently missing most of the luxuries. But no matter what, we didn't feel it was a real hardship to stick to the Army cooking.

Further, even if the food had been more inviting, I'm certain that we would've eaten with the Army. It was a sure way of building up the camaraderie which we enjoyed. We even welcomed the teasing because it meant we had been accepted. As I look back on this arrangement there is one aspect that seems surprising: the lack of any overt sexual cast. There was no thought of such a thing as sexual harassment. A little innocent and meaningless flirtation of the kind normally accompanying inter-sexual communication. That was it. It was several months before I even thought of the warning my mother had given me the night before I left home.

"Honey," she said, "you know there are a lot of wolves out there and you must be very careful." She looked at me very seriously with concern in her eyes.

I burst into laughter, which was not appreciated of course, and I had to explain at length that I was not laughing at the message but at her use of the word "wolves" which I had not expected to be in her vocabulary. Remembering this incident brought home to me how far removed from this view of hers was the actual existence I was living. The wolves were all wolfish in fun only, as when they called to each other, "Get away, you wolves" when they didn't want them cutting in at an officer's dance. I personally never came across one dressed in any other clothing.

"B.J. and Jane in Northern Ireland"

FIVE

A few days after our arrival in Ireland, we learned to drive the wrong-handed beast, the Clubmobile. Although it seemed all backward to us, we were glad to have the Bedford type with the Club mounted on the chassis, so that we could drive it ourselves, rather than the huge Greenliners which were not entrusted to the girls. We would not have traded our right to drive for anything. It was a precious manifestation of usefulness and independence, and something more; to see a woman driving a truck was so unusual in those days, that it was always a source of conversation and amusement to the men which meant we were getting a good start on our job without any more effort than it took to drive up to the outfit.

Jo and I each took half a day to get accustomed to the feel of this unwilling awkward machine. Under the tutelage of a warrant officer, we took it up one of the back untraveled roads, which meant almost any except the main highway and gave it full rein. Up and down these roads, hardly ever seeing another car, we trotted, pranced, cantered and reversed our vehicles until we'd mastered them. Our tutor who managed to have both of us end up at his outfit, laughingly admitted, "I promised the boys a closer look."

We felt we were fully versed in driving on the left hand side of the road, shifting gears with the left hand and remembering the inflated backside of the truck. A few days later, however, I had to take back my self-congratulation when it was my turn to drive. I learned the extent of my adaptability, and of Jane's tranquility, by coming to a complete impasse with a car coming directly at us from the opposite direction, before I realized what was wrong.

"You're driving on the wrong side of the road, B.J." Jane quietly told me.

What a patient mother she will make, I thought.

For the few days before Jo and I had our lessons, Jane had done the driving and the first day that we actually started on the job we were trained to do was an unusually bright one for January. Although we saw no snow to speak of that winter, (despite the continual griping about the cold) the days were often gray and drizzly, but this one dawned bright, inviting deep breaths of the clear air. We were scheduled to serve one of the companies of the regiment stationed all around our base in Rosstrevor. Sitting beside Jane, waving enthusiastically at every American we passed, I felt the elation inside as something to be treasured. We were about to be useful.

We drove about four miles down the road and turned into the gate of an old castle. Jane had told us that many of the outfits were using the many ancient castles to be found in Ireland for bases, and as we turned in the road all we could see was this one standing there alone on its knoll. It seemed completely out of place in the context of anything to do with the Army. Built of old stone, crumbling in parts, it had several spires reaching toward the sky surrounded by parapets; an imposing presence from afar. It looked like something that belonged on a slightly damaged cover of a fairy tale book.

But as we turned in and drove up the slight hill, this illusion was abruptly destroyed. Instead of a moat, the castle was surrounded by the typical Army digs. Nissen huts, trucks, jeeps, muddy roads, and the crowning touch: two long rows of men in olive drab uniforms standing near the mess hall with three garbage cans steaming with hot water for the mess kits.

"Are they waiting for us?" I asked.

With a slyly pleased look, Jane said, "Yes, this company is

especially appreciative. The officers are very cooperative about setting the time aside, and the men are always ready and waiting."

The men began beating their spoons on their tin cups when they saw the Clubmobile, and when Jo and I jumped out, an even greater din arose.

"New ones!" they shouted.

Nervously, I said something brilliant like "Hi" and waited for the question I knew to be coming: "Where ya from?"

Later, when I got to the Continent, I realized that one of the nicest things about Ireland was that after the first few weeks, we were asked that question only once in a while because by that time word as to where the Red Cross girls were from had gotten around. Almost a year later, while enduring the winter in France, we would spend a day with a can of white paint making a rough outline of the United States on both sides of the Clubmobile, designating where each of us was from with an X in rough approximation of our respective states. This enabled us to simply point when asked where we were from.

In the beginning of the tour, however, that question was not the banal treadmill it became, and I greeted it fondly as an easy way to start conversation, our stock in trade, knowing that our responses would start one of those spirited and seemingly fathomless discussions on the relative merits of the different states. It didn't help that most of them knew very little about the northwest except for the Oregon Trail.

"So—Where are you from?"

If I answered "Washington," I was apt to get "Oh, I have a sister who lives in Silver Springs," or something similar that would call for an explanation.

But if I said "Seattle," I usually got, "Oh yeh Oregon."

And when I answered that was the wrong state I'd get, "Oh, yeh. You're an apple knocker."

"No. The apple knockers are all on the other side of the mountains. And so is the snow, you know."

"Oh yeh, you get all the rain."

"Yes, but you don't have to shovel rain."

I learned to attack with vigor every part of the country except my own and felt I was getting along swimmingly. It was a heady experience to have everyone laugh at anything resembling a witty remark.

It would have helped with the banter to be from a state that lent itself to nicknames. For instance, there was a girl from Arkansas, stationed in a club fairly close to Rosstrevor who was dubbed "Arky". I kept getting this greeting, because she looked a great deal like me. But "Washy" is not something that comes naturally to the tongue. Jo was from California, so we were both a great disappointment, as I don't think there was over a handful of men from the West Coast in the whole division.

After we had emptied the coffee urns, Jane told me to go "mill around," as she handed me the "sweets tray," a little partitioned box with a handle in which we put the gum, life savers and cigarettes that were part of the Red Cross supplies.

I wandered around to different groups who stood drinking coffee. As I proffered my offering of sweets and small talk to such appreciative recipients, I remember feeling that this was a day never to be forgotten. The days leading up to this moment, days of doubt, homesickness, endless waiting and seeming futility disappeared, wiped out by this moment of true satisfaction with my role. I felt useful, full of the spirit of camaraderie that surrounded me, and aptly rewarded for the struggle.

But the slight pricking that all such balloons get soon came along and would repeat itself throughout the course of my career with the Red Cross. As I happily chatted with a group of GI's, telling them why I'd joined the Red Cross, trying to give them some sort of answer that approximated the truth without sounding sticky. (I was always loath to say anything like "I wanted to do something for my country." It sounded too pat. Yet to try to explain the impulses that brought me to this moment was too complicated for the kind of banter expected. Perhaps I couldn't explain it to myself. Perhaps I thought it would sound unfeminine to say something about the resistance to being left behind. Whatever it was, I found this question difficult to confront: sort of like being asked when you came to visit a sick person why you had come.)

At that moment a heavy silence fell over the men as if a stony blast of cold air had blown through the group. I truthfully didn't notice the bars on his shoulder until I looked more closely at the new addition to the group. The soldiers had all been talking at once but abruptly they clammed up, letting the Captain have the floor, and soon enough he and I were having a private conversation. The others fell back, listening with that resentfully respectful air accorded the brass, which was to become only too familiar. Desperately, I tried to ring them in again on the conversation, but they would have none of it. One by one, they drifted away, leaving the Captain and me to our private chat. A few more officers joined us and I stood there uncomfortably talking until we left. I wanted to run after the men, hold onto their coat sleeve and yell, "Don't go away. Please come back."

At the end of the day, as soon as we climbed into the cab, I asked Jane, "How do you keep that from happening? The GI's all walked away, leaving me with that officer, but what could I do?"

She laughed. To her it was an old story.

"The worst of it is," she said, "that you can't insult the officers or you'll just be cutting off your nose to spite your face."

"What do you mean?"

"We will have no men to serve," she said. "They don't have to accept us, you know. It's entirely up to the officers whether we're invited or not. And they won't appreciate your ignoring them."

I'd seen an inkling of this disparity while at Camp Pickett, but nothing I'd read about war, past or present, prepared me for the great gulf separating GI's and officers. A man's background became unimportant once the draft got him. What was important was the present label fastened on his uniform.

At first, I thought that by spending more time with the enlisted men than the officers I could satisfy everybody. I learned instead that I was more or less invisible to the GI's when I was with one of them, but if I went out with an officer, hardly a GI missed the sight. In my defense I tried explaining that I hadn't thought up the idea of commissions, and that I didn't judge a man by the tag the Army put on him, but that was inconceivable because that tag was so all-important to them. Besides, taking eight thousand men into your confidence was somewhat of a task. I was finally forced to realize that "she turns her smile on privates and generals alike," may sound democratic to generals and civilians, but to a private, a smile that had been flashed on anybody above a sergeant was tainted.

Since there were more enlisted men than officers, I tried ignoring the officers for a while, but when one such offended high brass reported me to the CIC (Counter Intelligence Corps) for sending uncensored pictures home—a misdemeanor of which I was innocent—I realized that Jane was right. It was dangerous to ignore an officer, because not only could he spirit the men away, he could spirit **you** away.

There was one circumstance in Ireland which was helpful, though. Our little hotel, the Great Northern, had been put off limits to the enlisted men, and the officers had their dances in the hotel proper. This meant that we could go to their dances by simply walking downstairs, thus avoiding any resentful eyes watching us get in and out of the jeeps. The only thorn in my conscience, then, was the orchestra. The officers always had their dances on Saturday nights and the same GI orchestra played for both GI and officer's dances.

I tried telling myself that I was imagining things, but it seemed to me that the greetings on Saturday nights from the orchestra smacked of the cold shoulder. One night, my worst imaginings were verified. I had flitted over to the leader to request a number, and stayed for a little conversation.

The band leader asked, "What is it about "String of Pearls" that you like so much? Remind you of an old boy friend. huh? It really isn't so hot to dance to." After a little more teasing, he got as far as asking me for a date.

"Oh, but I forgot," he said. "You're an officer's girl."

"What do you mean?" I said. "After all, don't you see me at two or three GI dances a week compared with one officers' dance.?"

"Yeah, but you seem to have a better time on Saturday night."

Maybe it was the liquor and cutting in on officers' night that provoked this observation. I suppose it might be thought that being passed from one pair of arms to another spells a good time for the girl. Actually it made for frustration, because dancing ability was usually in inverse correlation to rank. The higher the rank, the worse the dancer. Only a young lieutenant was apt to do the jitterbug (which was becoming my favorite) but a shavetail who cut in on a Captain, Major or Colonel, was either foolhardy or in his cups. So the night might start out well, but usually got bogged down to a slow walk.

It was not that I took the cold looks from the orchestra for personal animosity. I knew that these cold looks were not meant for me alone, but in the same way many men damn all women drivers when they see one make a mistake, these looks were vicariously meant for all Red Cross girls, and I felt as if I had the reputation of the whole group at stake on my shoulders.

One Sunday afternoon, I promised to go bicycling with a lieutenant. I did so with some hesitation because I had never learned to ride a bicycle well. Too many hills in Tacoma to make it worthwhile. But I felt fairly confident that I could manage a ride around Rosstrevor, where there were no really steep hills, so I accepted gladly, eager to explore the countryside up close instead of from the inside of the truck.

It was one of those jewel-like days which seem so much more dazzling in climates like the misty Irish one, because they're so rare. No coy hide and seek for the sun that day. It planted itself firmly in the heavens with only a few fleecy clouds as background. Such brilliance incited everything to turn an even deeper color in appreciation for the splendor and sunshine. As we turned off the main road, and came up over a small knoll to a view of the Lough, there came one of those flashes when you feel that surely the rest of the world must be barren to let nature concentrate her all in this particular spot. The over-sized rhododendron flaunted their just-opened blossoms as if reveling in their perfection and the rampant gorse answered by turning a brighter color of mustard.

The castle we picked as our destination was one of the many in Ireland built some eons ago, and left without concern to weather the elements. A huge old sow, which I delightedly mistook for a wild boar at first, rooted around in the straw and filth of the courtyard. My date and I spent some time wandering around the ruins, picking our way up the remains of some circular stone steps leading to little towers, nooks and crannies.

"I wonder where the little barefooted 'gossoons,' are," my companion said, using the Irish word we'd learned for 'children'. "Surely, there should be some of them playing at prince-courting-princess."

"Yes, I wonder, too," I said. "It makes you feel as if your childhood has been somewhat cheated. At least, In my part of the country anything over eighty-five years-old was made by nature; and neither trees nor people have anything like this to spur a child's imagination."

He chuckled absentmindedly, rumpling his close-cut hair, his eyes taking on that dreamy look of childhood nostalgia.

I left him to his remembrances for a while and poked around the castle, half expecting to find a "gossoon" somewhere around, but there was no one. Together then, we poked some more into crumbling circular staircases and little crevices that made one wonder what they might have one day held, and went on our way. Wandering on to the only tea shop open within twenty miles, we had our spot of tea and some fish and chips with vinegar before we started back.

Saturated with the brilliance of the day and the permanent atmosphere of the ruins, I felt far removed from the present and the Army. But, it all came back like a rude nudge of an elbow. There is one long, not very steep hill in Kilkeel leading past the only movie house in town on the way back to Rosstrevor. As we came to the foot of it, and dismounted our bicycles, a long line of uniforms extending all the way up the hill told us it was almost movie time. As we got closer, I recognized a few faces and started waving enthusiastically. But I soon lost my enthusiasm. They neither waved back nor said hello. Complete absence of wolf calls or whistles made their tacit and unanimous disapproval of my choice of companion very obvious. If only we had been going down, I thought. But no, we had to push our bicycles in front of us up the hill past this long row of silent, staring faces. By the time I had reached the top of the hill, my face was red more from embarrassment than physical exertion, and the phrase "running the gauntlet" seemed very meaningful.

I turned to my companion, the cause of all this, with some surprise to find that he was as embarrassed as I.

"I'm sorry," he murmured. "I should have thought of the show." His very young face, hardly yet bearded, was infused with a bright flush.

"I really had a good time," he said. "Too bad it had to end this way."

"Don't blame yourself," I said. "Blame the Army set up, I guess."

That was all I could think of to say, although I really felt sorry for him, and in other circumstances might have welcomed a second date.

But that incident stripped me of my optimism. From that day on, I never shook the guilt I felt conversing with officers. It was sort of like collaborating with the enemy: sometimes necessary for survival, but definitely punishable.

SIX

S ometimes during that first winter there were many times I felt my greenness was a distinct asset. It gave the men a great deal of pleasure to have so much to work with. However, in one place it was decidedly anything but an asset: the dance. Had I known how important this dance was going to be in my overseas duty I would have spent my last week in Seattle camped in an Arthur Murray studio learning to imitate a bobby soxer, for nobody could derive any pleasure from honing my Glen Miller free and easy dance style into the frenetic Jitterbug. I very quickly realized that this had to be corrected, for even when we just went out to serve, the Army seemed to be under a compulsion to keep vehement time to the music coming from our record player. There were, of course, some who had learned to dance in the same decade that I had, but their way of dancing did not lend itself to flailing around on the ground. They were always the ones on the fringes who watched while Youth took over. The decade separating eighteen from twenty-eight-year-olds became a real division on the dance floor, especially when the dance floor was the ground in front of our Clubmobile. Lacking any other partner, the jitterbuggers often danced with one another, but that had such a sad look, I was willing to breach the decade gap and make a fool of myself. In fact, I did it day after day those first few weeks.

   In the course of an ordinary serving day, invariably someone asks if we have "One O'clock Jump." if I've ever heard that record of Bunny Berrigan's? Someone else asks for "I Walk Alone" by Dinah Shore.

"Well," I say. We have Dinah, but we also have "Chattanooga Choochoo"

"Let's hear Dinah," comes a shout.

I instruct the guide on how to operate the portable phonograph in the Clubmobile, and he puts on Dinah Shore. Suddenly everyone looks so forlorn I instantly regret it and hope "White Christmas" is well hidden.

"Let's have something a little livelier," I say.

"Do you jitterbug?" five men demand at once when jivey music comes on.

"You might call it that," I say.

"Let's go," someone says hopping up to dance.

In my heavy stadium boots, I try to shuffle in coordination with an agile partner whose GI boots seem to impede him not at all. This is a particular frustration to me because I love to dance and when in college had found a strange satisfaction in being able to follow someone's contemplated step without having to think. I just relaxed into it. But the jitterbug was a different story; you're more on your own. And it had become the dance of the moment, without my noticing that my type of dancing was passe.

"What a disappointment we are to them," I wail to Jane with what breath I have left. "Here we are supposed to be the typical American girl, and what's their idea of a typical American girl? First and foremost someone who can cut a rug. And any little Irish girl who's still young enough can out jitterbug us by far.

Jane smiles her philosophical smile saying, "Let the Irish girls do it then."

She could be complacent about accepting things as they were, but not I. Maybe I was past the first flush of youth, but damn it I was going to learn to jitterbug. And I had plenty of opportunity. As I have indicated, there was a dance of sorts within striking distance every day of the week but Sunday. Some given by the outfits themselves, some by the Irish people for the Americans, and some by three nearby Red Cross Clubs. To most of these I hied myself along with the two Bridies and Kathleen from the hotel, and Jane or one of the other girls I could coax into a skirt. Around seven thirty of an evening, a jeep or truck arrived, having plucked Irish girls from all over the countryside, and off we went to the rumbling of the car accompanied by feminine chatter with a distinctly Irish accent.

In spite of this fraternization, I could never get very close to these Irish girls. They always treated me with great deference and respect helping me out of the jeep, and standing aside to let me get in first. Thus I found it difficult to throw off the feeling that I was chaperoning the affair. Once I mentioned to my dancing partner, who was a well-mannered, polished young man from South Carolina, that the Irish lasses must think it strange that none of the American girls jitterbugged very well.

With amazing honesty he said, "Yes, as a matter of fact, you all are a disappointment in many ways, for they also expected you to look like Ginger Rogers or Hedy Lamarr."

My first reaction was one of surprise that turned to amusement when I realized that I'd expected all of them to look like Maureen O'Hara. I could do little about looking like Hedy Lamarr, but to uphold the honor of my country, I had to learn to jitterbug. Whether they wanted to or not, those who could and would, took me over in a corner and educated my muscles to the down beat. There was one GI in particular they called "Pops"—because he was in his late thirties—who, in spite of his age, was a real expert. I called upon him often, and he responded willingly.

"Of course you're not too old to learn. Just look at me," he'd say, as he gave a little exhibition. Then he would settle down to showing me how to emulate him.

And fairly soon got results. I never got to the place where I could hop out on the floor with a flourish that said, "Look, this is the way we do it in the States," but I made real progress. And I became real fond of this captivating dance.

Sometimes in the midst of getting ready for a dance

contemplating a high heel shoe in one hand and a flat in the other, I would stop and ponder at the strange flood of circumstances that found me in the midst of a war more concerned over what to wear to a dance than I had been in the hey-day of my most frivolous undergraduate days.

I was not alone in this wonderment. In our private girl chats, the newcomers who came and went would echo my sentiments in one way or another. We were not very good at putting this feeling in words, because it was never clear in our own minds.

"Molly Pitcher would turn over in her grave," we'd say, coming home exhausted from a dance. Maybe we weren't sure exactly what Molly did during the Revolutionary War, whether it was taking over for her husband or bringing water to the troops, but we were certain she wasn't spending time so frivolously. To console ourselves we would say to each other, "After all, this is Occupation. Wait until we hit the real thing."

And in the meantime, these doubtful attitudes about the importance of the role we were playing were never maintained for very long. There were too many instances that made you feel it was important to be there. I was not being hyperbolic when I wrote home "Just being here is all it takes. They're so glad to see an American girl and hear American English spoken they just stand and look at you." And this was really true. I recall one time in particular, when we were persuaded to take an urn of coffee with some donuts to some GIs in the nearby Sick Bay. Two guys put the urn in a jeep and I walked alongside them down the road. One of them turned to the other and said, "She even smells different."

"Oh, you mean you can smell the donuts on me?" I asked.

"No, you smell feminine and American, something I haven't smelled for a long time." The intense look in his unfocused eyes convinced me that this was not just a "snow job."

Jane and I (and Jo or Elsa or Mary Lou) fared much better than the men, since we had much more freedom to control our own lives. And at night we could come home to a small coal fire in the grate for two shillings a day and the prospect of a luscious bed warmed with the little bed warmers called "pigs" for some reason, which were earthen jugs flattened to the size of a lunch box. Even though the "pigs" were put into the bed about six o'clock each night and were stone cold by the time we joined them, it was comforting to know that if you wanted to skip dinner you could have a warm bed. Not that we ever did skip dinner.

From our vantage point of comparative liberty and comfort, it's not surprising that we found life much less of a husk than the GI's did. No matter how patriotic, most of the men were understandably living a life not of their choosing, which they despised. Who wouldn't? When your every move was dictated to you as one of a horde of other men in the same exact uniform? They were thinking all the while about "home," and wishing they were there instead of this "lousy hole." While I could look around the Irish country with interest, to most of the men it seemed anything not American was obviously not good. For this reason I fretted over the magazine articles I sometimes got from home—the ones consistently describing the American soldier as an ambassador of good will, wisecracking his way into the hearts of people all over the world, and highlighting the treasure trove of better understanding he'd bring back to the States with him. This understanding was to be the indubitable result of experiencing the customs and mores of different cultures. Some of this was true of course. Children greeted anyone in an American uniform with, "Any gum chum?" And it was answered with a laugh and a generous hand-out.

But too often the GI's frustration and misery expressed itself in a hearty disdain. Using phrases like "this lousy hole" and "the lousy limeys" in front of natives does not make for a treasure trove of understanding. The wisecrack that my English date had told me that first night in London about American soldiers being "overpaid, oversexed, and over here" became old hat in short order, and actually carried with it great significance. Unpleasant though it might be, I thought it would behoove us to admit to the truth that the "ambassador of good will" was actually too often looking with jaundiced eye at anything and anybody not American to remotely merit this designation. He was not where he wanted to be and any place different from his home was consistently looked down upon.

On a later train ride to Scotland, I came across a Polish officer who was holding forth to some of us Americans how we did not appreciate that we were to be the leaders of the new world, and that we did not seem to have the necessary responsibility to take on the mantle. He said we hadn't really earned the right and weren't quite conscious of the privilege. He insisted we were too inclined to have fun and too arrogant towards the rest of the world. I wrote to my family about this incident saying, "I suppose to the rest of the world we seem frivolous because we laugh so much, but I would hate to be as serious as most of them are. Life seems such a burden to them, which it often is, I think. Well, I guess we are lucky but I do really think we could be a little more humble."

Perhaps these words sound very casual as if not much thought had been put behind them, but at that point in the United Kingdom I was doing a good deal of trying to puzzle out this problem. Why couldn't my fellow Americans see that the arrogant attitude so often expressed was not calculated to make for feelings of great empathy for us even among our allies? Did our arrogance come from an insecurity turned into bullying, or simple over-confidence? I could not say. But obviously the true admiration and envy we met with among our allies was too often fueled into ill-will.

Not that the actions of the American soldiers in WWII were alone responsible for the anti-American virus that we belatedly have come to recognize as having spread throughout the world. But they were certainly part of the seeds that we failed to observe; failure fostered by our desire to bring only good news. And today it seems particularly apparent that we are paying for our long history of inability to really look at how we're perceived in the eyes of the rest of the world. Because we were envied and imitated throughout other cultures and pride ourselves on our generosity, it was difficult to see beyond that.

Over the years while I harbored this sentiment I recall some dire warnings. One in particular—"The Ugly American," by William Lederer and Eugene Burdick, published in 1958. This book was a convincing picture of the situation in the third world where our dealings with people in these lands, whether as diplomat or corporate executive, were too often from our point of view only, paying no attention to their opinions, culture or knowledge. The end result—inefficiency plus a large measure of ill-will. The book was a best seller but for some reason the lesson went unheeded. Only recently has it been accepted in shocking surprise to most that a good portion of the rest of those on this planet, even those we count as friends, harbor a real dislike of the U.S. It surely would have been better if it had not been glossed over all these years.

No doubt the feeling of patriotism that comes over one at the sight of one's flag is a laudable emotion, but there is also no doubt that patriotism can easily turn into a dark nationalism. "My country right or wrong" is a dangerous motto, as Japan and Germany taught us so thoroughly and disastrously.

SEVEN

F lushed with the victory of conquering the Jitterbug and the cold germs I had been skirmishing with all winter, I greeted the spring with new-found confidence and a new appreciation of the emerald of the "emerald isle." The lush greens of all different hues seemed to be trying to outdo each other in size and vigor. And even the most disgruntled GI had to remark on the beauty of the tremendous rhododendron bushes and the vibrant color of their lavish blooms. Even more of a harbinger of the season was the crop of the new little lambs which appeared everywhere. One morning I saw a tiny girl with her toes sticking out of worn sandals, lovingly holding a new little lamb in her arms that was almost as big as she was. You could see this was a normal, happy experience for the little child. As usual, I regretted that I did not have my camera.

Since getting close to the main action of the war was our ultimate goal, Jane and I handled our day-to-day traffic in donuts in Rosstrevor and environs with one eye cocked on the Continent, determined to meet the future well-primed.

"You never can tell what we may be called upon to do," we said holding onto our hopefully heroic conception of our role.

We had to be asked only once if we'd like to try our hand shooting carbines. These were the rifles with the least amount of kick, so they would do less damage to our tender shoulders. From then on it was a cold heart that got past our pleading looks on the way to the rifle range. Conveniently, this range backed up against our hotel, so the donut business didn't suffer at the expense of our foray into rifle shooting.

"From dough girl to 'doughgirl' (we knew that soldiers were called "doughboys" in WWI) in nothing flat," we quipped as we took turns washing the flour off our hands and heeling an expedition to the rifle range. Here we took our place at individual stations like a driving range and aimed at the bull's eye in the middle of graduated circles at the other end.

This coaching was the sort of sharpening up the men gloried in dispensing, and we furnished them with many happy moments. Although the first time I fired this supposedly innocuous rifle, it almost knocked me off my feet, thereafter I managed to hold my own. Scores were given like darts: the nearer the eye the higher the score, and naturally it took me some time to even come near the bull's eye. Jane would come back with scores little better than mine, and when the men compared our scores with theirs, they complimented us with gales of good-hearted laughter.

"Oh, wow, you're getting up there. Another six months and you might get a bull's eye," they would say gleefully. I almost hated to show any improvement for fear their enthusiasm would wane.

Not content with this type of "sharpening up," we looked around for more fertile fields in which to sow our seeds of preparedness. Next on our list was the Battle Indoctrination Course. This was the course where you crawled under live ammunition that flew by a few feet above your head. With the advent of spring, this became quite a popular maneuver among the different outfits and we were frequently asked to furnish our refreshments to wind up the affair. On one such occasion we decided that at an opportune time, instead of driving up at the last minute in our Clubmobile, we should go through the course with the men and serve our donuts and coffee afterwards. Thus, the next time one of the more amiable Colonels came to us with a request to meet the group after the running of the course, we made our own request.

"So, you want to become inured to crawling under live

ammunition, do you?" said the Colonel. "I don't believe you'll ever be called upon to use this practice." His pleasant smile told us that he was not averse to the idea.

"Maybe not." I piped up. "But you never know. It'll probably be good for our character at least"

"I guess there's no reason you shouldn't if you really want to," he said, giving us directions for meeting the outfit at a castle we were familiar with, a few miles off the main road to Kilkeel.

That night, dressed in our helmets, fatigues and GI boots, feeling very true to our hardy ancestry, we drove our Clubmobile over to the appointed castle. It was just turning dark, when we got there to find the trucks all lined up with their cargo of manpower ready to go to the range. We sought out the Colonel for directions, and he told us to leave our Clubmobile and ride down in the trucks. He was very busy being Colonel but not too busy to carefully tuck us into the cabs of two trucks, Jane in one and me in another. My driver, when he saw me, acted as if he were having hallucinations, or maybe it was just his short, short haircut that gave him a permanent expression of surprise. But by the time we reached our destination—a wide, flat forsaken spot covered with little green growth of any kind—he had rallied to the point of being very protective, having doled out all the advice that people had repeated to each other for some time.

"Now you know, it really is live ammunition," he said. "So in case you see a rattlesnake or something like that, for God's sake stay down on the ground. You'll probably want to stand up but never, never do that."

"I thought St. Patrick or somebody drove all the snakes out of Ireland," I mused.

"Well, maybe a rat," he said. "Betcha you're afraid of rats, yeah? Well, forget it. Better to be bitten by a rat than a bullet."

He carried on for some time, but I was only half-listening, trying to remember if I had ever seen a snake in Ireland, (after all, in my homeland of similar climate and makeup there were occasional snakes) and so paid no attention to his next warning, as he stopped the truck.

"I think you'd better wait here for the Colonel," he cautioned. "Why wait for the Colonel?" I said, only half heeding his concerned tone and nonchalantly slamming the door behind me.

Without a worry, I started around the truck, but before I had gone two feet, my insouciance turned into astonishment laced with puzzled indignation. The men were swarming out of the trucks, shouting and yelling—the usual familiar scene. But there was something new, and at that point, very unfamiliar: language I knew existed but never heard. A language which really rocked my ears that were attuned to nothing worse than "sonofabitch," and that only infrequently. What had happened to the comforting power of the presence of women to stifle this language? It may be difficult for those brought up on today's movies to imagine the assault this language presented to my ears. But at that time, such phrases were never, never used in the presence of a woman, at least in polite society, as we used to say. And here everyone was shouting the same sort of expressions, which had that strange power to shock. I realize now that words are not inherently evil. The word "shit" and "fuck" have within them no innate immorality. Change the middle vowel and they become perfectly respectable. Think of "bloody" which was completely innocent to us, but not at all to the English, at least back then. Words, only words, and by now most of us are numb to them; they have lost all power to even startle, serving only to express bad taste. But at that time these words, because they were forbidden, had a very strong power to completely shock.

As I stood there with my smug little world teetering, I realized with sickening certainty that there were actions to go with the language. It seemed as if every man, upon getting out of the trucks, probably due to a little nervousness, had to relieve himself right then and there—and not even with the benefit of bushes! What had happened? I looked around for Jane but couldn't find her. Then it came to me. The night was completely moonless and In the late twilight, her helmet and GI clothes made her completely indistinguishable from any of the men. They didn't know we were there!

Jane and I found each other by instinct, afraid now to speak, and raced down the line of trucks to the Colonel. We found him, identifiable by his pitiful state of confusion and embarrassment. He, too, had not thought about the dark night and how we'd be camouflaged. He got the men in formation quickly, sending a hissing word down the line.

"For Christ's sake, watch it. We've got women with us tonight."

Before any of this had time to travel my nervous system, we were all down on our stomachs wriggling along under the colorful, exploding sky, I, very much impeded by my helmet which kept sliding down over my eyes like a washtub set over me. Whenever I could push it back long enough to see the colorful flares above, I would find myself forgetting to wriggle, mesmerized by the scene. I lost Jane during one of these interludes, and when it was over, picking myself off the ground I fell in beside a man who expressed himself with fierce indignation. What I want to know," he said, "is where the hell are the fucking women who are supposed to be here?"

"Here. Here. I'm one of them," I said.

He promptly vanished, and I kept up a running conversation with no one in particular about nothing at all the entire way back to the truck. Once in the truck en route to our Clubmobiles, the driver who had been so voluble before seemed to have lost his voice. He didn't say much, not even "I warned you."

Upon returning to the castle, we changed into our battle dress as quickly as possible and presented ourselves inside our opened Clubmobile with our coffee and donuts, as if we had been there all the time.

This incident might have been a deterrent to our fondness for "sharpening up," but I was so in love with this idea that I kept looking for more opportunities. I did notice a new-found hesitancy in Jane, which I deplored and undertook to correct. We had gone out to serve some twenty miles north of our base near one of those surprising Irish lakes. These lakes always amazed me because there were no signs of any use. No cabins, no boats, no concessions. It seemed no one ever thought of them in terms of recreation. And yet they were beautifully clear and inviting.

This spring evening our objective was an outfit on maneuvers, and we found them bedded down in a thick growth of underbrush, not far from the lake's edge, lolling around in a scene that might have presented all the romance of a gypsy camp. A fire was going for the evening meal and if someone had just been playing a violin near the pristine little lake, it would have made a beguiling site. But being the Army, the overall feeling was not one of romantic adventure but boredom, which Jane and I proceeded to try and dispel.

Donuts and coffee helped, but that night we didn't have our music. (Because of the roads which were two ruts on each side of a high crown we had to abandon our Clubmobile for a jeep.) We had just about exhausted the conversational possibilities of one state versus another, when the sergeant, ready for any diversion, spoke up.

"Let's teach these gals to throw a hand grenade," he said.

"That's a great idea," I said.

"Oh, I don't know," Jane said, hanging back.

Nothing about the idea appealed to her, I could see, but I cajoled her along in my eagerness. The men loved showing us how to pull out the plug at the right time and throw it quickly. Otherwise, it will go off in your hand, they warned us. They liked making it sound dangerous, of course. But It looked easy enough, and I took the thing in one hand, pulled out the plug and without any hesitation got it over one of the ubiquitous little stone hedges. After I had tried a few without any damaging effects, I insisted that Jane try it.

I could see no chance of any danger. The little hedge, despite its low height, seemed ample protection even if the grenade only made it to the other side. Knowing Jane's strength, I could see no reason to feel any qualms and watched with satisfaction as the grenade she threw sailed high into the air. Unfortunately though, fate had placed a tree directly in its path. Upon impact, it exploded in the air. In itself, this would not have been a problem, the explosion being far enough away to leave all of us intact. However, the cap of the grenade ricocheted off the tree, sending back into the watching group tiny, sharp pieces of tin. Two men standing there were abruptly goaded into yelps of pain.

They were not badly hurt, fortunately, and Jane did not blame me (audibly, anyway) but her chagrin was only surpassed by mine. The medic soon had the wounded boys fixed up, but this event was enough to dampen even my ardor for "sharpening up" a little, and as for Jane, she refused to have anything more to do with any firearms. I did not try to egg her on to any more such events, and actually there was little opportunity.

For, as the weather grew warmer and warmer in April, rumors of the prospective invasion began to crop up along with the daffodils. Naturally, everyone knew that there was going to be an invasion—all these thousand and thousand of troops sitting in the United Kingdom had to be for the operation which was to come. No one, as we would learn later, even the commanders who had not yet decided, knew where it would take place. It was a long time afterwards that the names "Utah Beach," "Omaha Beach," where the Americans landed on "D Day" in the "Operation Overlord" became the familiar names they are today.

Still, we knew something was about to happen, and any slight change in routine or equipment brought a stir of excitement and a quick tension. Mornings in the Clubmobile were frequently enlivened by someone dropping in and asking excitedly, "Did you hear? Won't be long now?"

"What? What?" we'd ask.

"The P. O. number's been changed."

Or: "There are to be no more equipment issues to be sent here."

Or: "No more personnel to be sent here."

Any alteration in the daily routine was deemed significant for a short time. But then we'd pass this news along to the next man who came for a donut, and he'd say, "Oh don't kid me. This division will never get off this lousy island."

And even in the face of reason, this seemed the more credible belief, so boredom would once again set in, only to be relieved the next day with a new rumor.

With May, however, came undeniable confirmation that change was indeed imminent. We were ordered to close down operations for one week and report to Newcastle. This was the base for the Red Cross girls with the other half of the Fifth Division, and arrangements had been made for the Army to give all the Red Cross girls in this section of Ireland a really worthwhile bit of "sharpening up." We were to learn to drive the two and one-half ton GMC trucks which we would be using on the continent. About eight of us from the surrounding area convened there and the next morning reported to a lieutenant with a clipboard in his hand, whose expression betrayed that he didn't know whether to be aggrieved or elated with this assignment as he delegated each of us to a specific truck and driver.

For these men, too, teaching women to drive was a distinct cross between a reward and a punishment. At first, they seemed unable to decide whether it was sheer heaven to be in the company of an American woman for a week or sheer hell to be teaching her to drive. In the end, they responded with typical rivalry, each wanting to show that his charge could outdo the others.

About the third day, my particular GI, a lanky bean pole-type, looked at me with an expression of confidence. His deep blue eyes looked full of delight as if giving someone a welcome surprise.

He rubbed his sharp chin thoughtfully as he said, "You know, when I first saw you, I thought you would never be able to drive this truck. After all, your legs are hardly longer than a chicken's. But you know what?"

He stopped when he saw my mouth open in indignation.

"I was only kidding," he said. "I mean to say that now, guess what, I think you're good enough that I can teach you to shift without double clutching."

As a matter of fact, the ease with which these six-by-six trucks handled compared to our balky English Bedfords was a real source of delight. Nonetheless, shifting one of them was quite a different maneuver from flicking the gear on today's automatics. I should have been quite content to go along double clutching in the mundane manner for the rest of my days but in the face of such praise I didn't dare question the practicality of such skill. Eventually, when we all came home exhausted from the day's work, it came out that all of us had been put through the same paces: shifting without double clutching. That was why it was so difficult to manage to be the last in line (in order to pick up the necessary speed); everyone was vying for last place.

After the driving lessons came the maintenance. We were taught how to take care of these trucks: to grease them, to water them, to put chains on them. We all got through that ok, but then came changing the tires. I'm glad to say that we all tried, but most of us looked at the crowbar with misgivings. We could get it on the bolt but only a couple of the girls could get it to budge without standing up on top of the crowbar and jumping up and down on it. We fervently hoped (correctly) that we would not be called on to do this again after we passed our tests. After we finished with truck maintenance, we went on to map reading and operation of the field ranges.

Oh, those field ranges! Definitely not good examples of the reputed technical prowess of the U.S.—they were the regular GI field stoves, real weapons of horror. After each use they had to be taken apart, piece by piece, and each piece had its particular tool. Upon littering the floor with tools and pieces, you had to match the piece with its tool, then blow, scrape, brush and put them all together again. Then you filled it with gasoline and pumped up the pressure again, forty pounds with a bicycle pump. I wondered if the Army cooks in combat would have more success with them than we did. I don't think they ever did. I know they would like to have ditched them if ever possible.

Fortunately, we all passed the tests with flying colors and Jane and I came back to our cozy little hotel and Company I, very proud and ready to show off our prowess with the GMC's at the slightest provocation. Now, we knew that it could not be much longer. With excitement and anticipation we pictured ourselves soon driving onto the continent with one of these functional vehicles. I had been back only a week or so, when Eva, the supervisor at Belfast, whom I had never seen but who would become very familiar within a few weeks, called to say that I was being transferred to Newcastle and promoted to Captain. The rest of the contingent there was being recalled to London (more rumor material) and there were two new girls coming so, as a veteran of sorts, I was to show them the ropes. Despite the fact that I was being promoted, I found this disheartening news for it meant that I had to leave Jane, Rosstrevor and Company I. True, there was some satisfaction in the recognition that I had survived long enough to become a Captain, but this label in the Red Cross was very different from the Army's. The one with the most experience became the Captain, and that was that. There was no recognition, such as another bar on one's shoulder. Still, there was, perched on my shoulder, the young homesick girl I had been just six months earlier whispering into my ear, "I knew you could do it."

In less than ten days I was again called to the phone at the Slieve Donard Hotel, this time to be told I was headed for London with Jane. This, then must be the real call. No doubt Ireland would soon be stripped of Americans. Back at Rosstrevor I went through a second session of fond farewells, only this time with the big difference—"see you over there." Words loaded with a significance only dimly understood, and impossible to be prepared for. No doubt for most of the men they signified relief from boredom mixed with dread. For myself, while I thought I could understand those feelings I read on the faces of the GI's I counted as friends, I knew I could never fully comprehend them. My view of all that was happening had to be limited by my role, just as later on the continent, I realized the men back in rear headquarters could not fathom the feelings of the front line infantry-men.

These final farewells finally accomplished, I prepared for bed that night taking a long look around our room with its little coal grate and the blue and white wall paper that had become so boringly familiar. It was like saying goodbye to an old taken-for-granted friend, knowing a chapter had been closed, full of wonderment about the morrow.

EIGHT

T he next morning towards the last of May, Jane and I
hitched a ride to Belfast, then hitched another ride on
a C-47 cargo plane and landed a few hours later in London. This
was two weeks before D Day, June 6, 1944, and the excitement
that had hold of London was palpable. Not that anyone knew
when or where "it" was to happen, or exactly what "it" was. But
there was no doubt that the recent grouping together of thousands
and thousands of English, American, Canadian and Anzacs
(Australian and New Zealanders) troops, was in preparation for
some kind of invasion. This was what we had been waiting for.
But the success obviously depended upon the attack being kept a
surprise. That accounted for a certain excitement combined with
solemnity overtaking everyone.

Looking back, I wonder at the complete confidence that all
Americans displayed. Perhaps because we hadn't lost a war? Merely
looking at a map of the United Kingdom and the Continent
made it clear that it would no doubt be someplace across the
English Channel. Still, it was well known that the only such
invasion attempted before across this water—at Dieppe (in August
of 1942)—had been a complete failure. Moreover, if Hitler
hadn't attempted it in reverse when he had all of Europe under
his thumb how did everyone have such supreme assurance? But
they did.

When we arrived at the Red Cross Headquarters, it was with
some uncertainty that we reported at the front desk. Although

we felt quite sure that we must have been called back to London
to prepare for going to the Continent, we had no guarantee that
was to be our destination. A kindly older woman at the desk
looked up our names and then told us with a certain flourish—
in the de rigeur solemn-but-excited tones—to report to a room
down the hall. There we were greeted politely by a younger woman
with a the same pleasant but grave demeanor. She told us in a
manner appropriate to giving us a prize that we were being assigned
to groups heading to Zone 5, wherever that was to be, and handed
us circular patches with a red 5 in the center that we were to wear
on our left sleeve. This meant nothing to anyone not in the Red
Cross, but we wore our patches as if they were a pair of pilot's
wings. We had made it.

Jane and I insisted that we wanted to stay together, but were
told that since I was now a Captain, we couldn't be on the same
Clubmobile. We were assured, however, that we would be
assigned to the same group. The dates of departures depended on
the fateful, but unknown D-Day. In the meantime, we were given
short assignments out of London, remaining on call more or
less. Since I hadn't had a leave in the nearly six months I'd been
overseas, I took mine at once and spent the week getting acquainted
with London. Jane was to stay in London to teach some of the
girls who'd missed the course in maintaining the GMC trucks,
so she and I covered the spots all sightseers head for, including a
side trip to Stratford-on-Avon, where we were naturally
accompanied by several stray GI's.

I recall that day paddling along the famous river, marveling
at the past—the past all around me. A certain timelessness was in
the air, the early summer tranquility like an eternal lullaby. I knew
that for all history the insects had always droned lightly, that the
water had always lapped softly against the banks of the Avon,
and perhaps it was here that Shakespeare sat and thought in blank
verse. In some ways, that tour of old England, from under half-
closed lids in the shadow of the past, seemed more real than the
actuality of the present: the present accompanied by unknown

men, unknown and unknowable, yet so familiar as American-accented uniforms. We kidded about the invasion, the imminent impossibility, which had to be just days away in tones both flippant and awe struck and I wondered what the great bard would've thought of the modern counterpart to his Prince Hal, the young reluctant warrior of "King Henry IV." Youth must not have been so young.

Another vivid memory of that tour in England was the day that we heard General Patton speak to a full battalion of the Army gathered for the occasion. A group of Red Cross girls was given the honor of being seated on the platform as the General gave them a pep talk for the battles to come. A line of folding chairs for about ten of us was set up behind the general as he pranced on the makeshift stage. This meant we were facing the huge audience unable to hide our reactions. I think most of us ended up looking at the floor.

I wrote to my family, "Old 'Blood and Guts' certainly deserves his name." After describing the embarrassment that we girls felt on this occasion having to be on display to the men as we reacted to the speech, I ended with the remark, "Guess he doesn't think the RC girls are ladies." Today that remark makes me grimace with its prudish connotation. Did I expect him to use proper language just because we were there? Well, maybe not, although as I have said, we did not hear it from the men if they knew we were there. No, but his whole address was about what was soon to be expected in the way of combat. What surprised was the vivid way the bombastic general acted out, with vivid gestures, the elation one should feel as he plunged a bayonet into the bowels of the evil foe. With enjoyment! ("This is the enemy. Why are we fighting? Because we like a good fight.") I was aware that his purpose was to goad the soldiers into the right mood to kill, a difficult task, but it still stunned. This reaction was recalled to me recently when a friend, in a discussion of the war, reported her husband's shock back at that time, coming home on leave from his first training camp, "Why, do you know what they are

training us to do? Well, to kill somebody." I thoroughly
understood his dumbfounded surprise.

A few days after my leave was over the news came on the
radio. The troops were on their way across the English Channel.
The invasion had started! People stayed glued to the radio, but
the success of the operation remained in doubt for hours. The
news was scarce, due in part to the necessity to keep Hitler in the
dark. How hard it was to imagine what was going on on those
beaches just across the channel. Now we are fully aware of the
supreme effort it took to secure a foothold as witnessed in all the
graphic display since then, but at the time we could only try to
imagine.

I thought back to two and a half years earlier, the day of Pearl
Harbor and the great difference. Now there was no shock, just
excitement and prayerful anticipation of success. In fact, when I
rushed to downtown London wanting to be in the midst of the
excitement, I found none to speak of: two American soldiers in
Piccadilly Circus throwing their hats in the air; that was the only
demonstration I saw all day. Of course England had been drained
of most of the troops, and perhaps, mixed in with the prayerful
hope, was relief at having their country mostly to themselves
again.

A few days later I was given the shocking news that I was to
be sent to Scotland. It sounded so far away and in such an utterly
different direction from which I was aiming, that I was too
stunned to protest, in anything but terms too polite to be noticed,
that I didn't want to leave Jane. I said goodbye to her, confident
that I should see her again on the continent though I never did.
Our paths never crossed at all and once more I experienced that
fleeting, transient camaraderie, as strong as it was short-lived,
that was part of war.

I set out for Scotland with a personable, new girl from Iowa,
who broke into repeated raptures gazing out the window. Her
face would light up at the sight of a group of Angus cattle, because

it reminded her of home. I had to admit they made for an interesting landscape, the black animals standing out in contrast to the varied-hues of green, although I thought the neat patchwork-like hills behind them was not much like my picture of her home state. She also taught me Iowa's thoroughly corny and wonderful song, "That's Where the Tall Corn Grows." That reassured me about the vision of her state I had in mind.

Our destination was a place called Greenock and Gourock, little Siamese-twin towns, hugging the west coast of Scotland on the Firth of Clyde. It's hard to tell where one stops and the other begins; I assume that is why they are always spoken of as one. Their claim to fame was that the Queens were built here. (the two original liners named the Queen Elizabeth and the Queen Mary—the largest in the world at that time.) These two ships, plus some smaller ones, docked in Greenock and Gourock off-loading cargoes of American troops, and it was our job to meet the soldiers with our wares. This operation was called ranging, just why I don't know.

Our base was the home of a Scotch woman whose husband was at sea. She was a short woman with a rather hooked nose, but a brilliant smile, and seemed very happy to have something to do while her husband was gone long stretches at a time. To my delight she lived up to my idea of the Scotch by describing almost everything as "wee" whenever it was anywhere close to appropriate. She tried to make us feel at home, and indeed it was more like home than any other time overseas. It was a really pleasant interlude in a real home with real beds and a living room where we could sit and talk or play bridge. Because of the intervals between ships and because we didn't have to make donuts we had more time to ourselves. We even squeezed in sightseeing trips to Edinborough and Loch Ness.

In the meantime we greeted the troops coming from the States. There were as many as fifteen Red Cross girls there at one time and we needed that many, considering the number of donuts handed out to the thousands of soldiers debarking from only one of the Queens. When we were told by the Quartermaster

Corps that a ship was scheduled to come in, we would pick up the previously ordered donuts at the bakery, take them to the docks and spend many greasy hours putting them on the trays. Fortunately, a corps of Scotch women, acting as volunteers, would meet us there to make the vast quantity of coffee needed. Inevitably, the "hurry up and wait" regime of the Army made for a long wait between the time set for debarkation and the actual event. The towns furnished different bands to march up and down the platform in welcome and we could count on them waiting with us. We always hoped for the kilt and bagpipe variety because during the long hours of waiting, we'd get the band members to teach us the Highland Fling. We never became very proficient at it though; it may not look so energetic, but it was more exhausting than the jitterbug.

The anticipation had its payoff; it made the final event more exciting as the ships arrived and the troops started coming up the dark causeway. Loaded down like pack horses and still in formation, they marched onto the empty trains ready to take them to their destinations. We gathered and waited—always full of the expectant possibility that there would be a familiar face among them. This happened to me only once, but girls from the East were far luckier. Every so often, there'd be the whoop of recognition. Whether it was an old friend, or a casual acquaintance, the greeting was never anything but wildly enthusiastic.

The men always looked a little bewildered as their eyes adjusted to the light. Even when they could see us, they laughed uncertainly when we shouted at them. We didn't understand the laugh at first, but learned later that this being their first contact with foreign soil, they expected us to be Scotch lassies, and were surprised by the familiar American accent. They did not yet recognize our uniforms.

I remember my surprise the first time I said, "Welcome to the ETO" to a group of them.

"What's that?" they chorused.

"The European Theater of Operations," I said, feeling very much a veteran. "And you are in it. Aren't you 'nervous in the service'?"

When the first train was full, upon a signal from the Lieutenant of the Transportation Corps we would run—not walk—with our trays of donuts and huge pitchers of coffee. Working against time we divided up, two to a car, and raced down the aisles, talking, explaining, shouting, pouring, saying, Seattle, Washington, or Minot, North Dakota, or Montgomery, Alabama. Then, we'd hustle back to the dock and the Scotch women for more coffee and donuts. It was important to remember were you had left off, ignoring outstretched arms for refills. Smiling, always smiling, we would ultimately run alongside the train as it pulled out, tossing donuts through windows and pouring coffee into outstretched cups if we could.

As the train pulled out, another pulled in, and the process started all over again, until thousands of men were off-loaded from the ships and on their way. It took hours and hours, sometimes whole days, and by the end of this operation, we girls were greasier than our donuts.

Sometimes a boatload of German prisoners would be loaded onto the empty ships to go back to the States, and it was then that the ambivalence about war and humanity surged up in me. As the prisoners came out into the daylight, they'd look up to see the ship and a smile would cross their faces when they saw the American flag, rather than that of another country. Often a GI guard or MP would be standing there and say something like, "Yeah, ya better smile you lucky dog. I gotta stay here. You don't."

We girls would laugh uncertainly. Some might suggest giving them any donuts we had left over, and others would say, "No Jerry's going to get a donut from me." But there were plenty of us who, reared on the books about World War I that stressed the common humanity of soldiers, were far less ready to voice definite opinions. At least, I was tongue-tied by the confusing ambivalence that came and went again and again in different situations where we encountered "the enemy" but felt tugged by the sense of humanity.

The ships' schedules were very irregular. Some days there were no ships, some days two or three at once. Sometimes they came in at night, sometimes in the morning. Since there were no troops in town, except the handful with the Transportation Corps, we had no one else to serve, but we did get to two other bases in Scotland. One was a naval base, Roseneath, about fifty miles away. The other was the 50th General Hospital, which already had many casualties from the channel beachheads, men with broken bones or other injuries that would take time to heal but not severe enough to warrant sending them home. I could never get over the feeling talking to them that it didn't seem right to send them back. They did not talk much about their prospects of going back, but I recall one GI, with a cast on his right arm and left leg, in the midst of the usual banter, who started out jokingly, "Well, all I can say is I hope they get this damn war over soon. One purple heart is more than enough for me." And ended a little bitterly, "But I guess I don't have any say in the matter."

Since this was June in Scotland, we could start out at seven p. m. for these operations and still have four or five hours of daylight until the end of a shift. We'd come home at midnight just as the sun was setting and dash to bed so that we could get to sleep before the dawn broke an hour later. The sun did such a short fade-out that if we didn't rush, all the birds would be gathered outside our window, greeting the dawn. I still wonder about those birds. How did they ever get enough sleep?

Altogether, I spent about five weeks in Scotland. Girls kept coming and going, but there were a few of us slated for the Continent who just seemed to stay on and on. We were alone together more than any other time in the Red Cross because of the lack of nearby troops, and the intervals between the ships. Since we had no way of making donuts and ordered them from a bakery, we had some free time. Certainly it was the easiest portion of my sojourn as far as physical work. Nevertheless, those of us slated for the continent had the feeling we were just biding time in a way, waiting for Zone 5. We were anxious to get started. As the weeks dragged on I became more and more impatient. By now, we kept hearing the news that the invasion had gained a foothold and the troops were on their way across Normandy. The news was not very specific, of course, since Hitler had to be kept in the dark about the details of how many and where. but there was no doubt that the Allies were gaining ground. It must be time for us in Zone 5 to be crossing the channel. Had the Red Cross Command forgotten us? From the remote corner of Greenock and Gourock, it seemed possible. New arrivals made us feel even farther away, bringing news of the advent of the horrendous "buzz bombs" falling on London, and finally even the departure of some of the Clubmobiles across the channel. This was too much. We called London HQ. No, they hadn't forgotten us. Those of us who'd been there the longest were told to report to London within the next few days in staggered pairs.

NINE

Back in London, the first day was spent at Red Cross Headquarters in Grosvenor Square getting acquainted with my group. Altogether there were ten alphabetical groups of Clubmobiles sent to the continent, with only three still to go: Groups H, K, and L. Each group consisted of eight Clubmobiles named after familiar American cities, landmarks or people. I was to be Captain of the "Cedar Rapids," a part of Group "H". Under this letter of the alphabet a group of thirty two girls gathered together expectantly. We knew we were going to spend an unknown period of time in close contact, so naturally we looked at each other hoping to see a familiar face. I looked around for Jane confident that she would be there, but she was nowhere to be seen.

Our supervisor, Eva, turned out to be the one in Belfast that we had missed on the first day in Ireland. She was a rather raw-boned blonde of Swedish extraction, capable looking with easy take-charge attributes of authority. She was busy trying to answer everyone's question, and when I got to her she told me almost apologetically that unfortunately Jane had already left with another group. It wasn't her fault of course so I swallowed the disappointment, recognizing that as part of Red Cross life in the ETO. Looking around at the group I found no familiar faces. I had never seen any of them before, including the two assigned to my crew: Jean, from Massachusetts, and Doris, from upstate New York. Naturally we looked at each other with curiosity knowing that we would be a threesome in close contact with each other for who-knew-how-long. Jean was a bouncy sort of person with short blond hair framing a round affable face. Much later I was to learn that this two years overseas was the only time in her life that she wasn't slim. "Must've been the donuts," she said when I commented on how thin she was at our one reunion. Doris had dark red hair down to her shoulders and a light sprinkling of freckles to match her hair. I learned very soon that her personality was not at all the temperamental kind associated with redheads. No one would have called her "Carrot Top". She was very earnest and worked hard at being a good sport.

The group was divided into two Sections H1 and H2, and was to convoy in order when we moved together. Our "Cedar Rapids" was the second one in the second section with H2/2 painted front and back, and meant we would follow the sign H2/1 painted on the truck ahead of us for a good many stretched out kilometers across the continent. That way we could not lose anyone. And it did not take long to discover that the division of the two sections was more than just physical. The first half—the H/1's—had almost all been with the Second Armored Division somewhere in the south of England for the last few months and were very attached in loyalty to that outfit. According to them, the whole group was supposed to be attached to this Second Armored Division, which made me wonder for a few minutes. How could we all be attached to one division when it required only two Clubmobile in Ireland?

Compared with the cohesion of the first half, our section had very diffuse loyalties; I was the only one from the Fifth Division, which made me miss Jane even more. We could have commiserated together over missing the Fifth, even though there had been no expectation of anything else.

Our Clubmobiles were parked in a large field on the outskirts of the city which we visited several times a day, getting them ready for the fateful day of crossing. These trucks were the ones we had received our training for in Ireland: the regular Army 2-1/2 ton GMC. My non-mechanical mind was surprised to learn now that the tag "2-1/2 ton" referred to the capacity—the weight it could hold—rather than its own weight, which was eight tons, to be exact. The chassis was an improved and embellished version of the one we'd had on the Bedford in Ireland with more space and more cupboards packed to the hilt with supplies. We had to take inventory of these supplies, which meant crawling over folding chairs, a card table and a long wooden bench to get to the barrels of flour, huge cartons of sugar, coffee and lard, all stacked in the back. Each Clubmobile had a small trailer attached with different necessary equipment—generators, water tank, tents and other supplies. Our training in Ireland did not include these trailers but I soon learned that backing them up was a real art. If you wanted the trailer to go left you aimed right. Considering this difficulty, we had very few accidents over the next eighteen months even with the trailers tagged on behind.

For the two weeks or so that we were in London preparing to cross the channel we became acquainted, not happily, with the buzz bombs we had heard about. They always came at night with so little warning that you didn't have time to run to a shelter, as with the previous bombings. I know everyone had the same feeling I had when you heard their noisy little engines coming by your bedroom. "Keep going, keep going. please keep going." The reaction was automatic because you knew that if the whirling stopped it was your doom. At the same time you had the feeling of being selfish to wish it on someone else. So you just buried your head deeper under the covers.

Finally, the day came when an Army truck picked us up—us and our luggage, bed roll and foot locker apiece—and we made our last trip to our vehicles. At this point, there were now only thirty one of us; one girl having decided to return to England to get married.

"Do you have your K rations? Helmets? Gas, water and air checked? Now stay in your vehicles!" Eva came by shouting orders from her jeep.

We were off. Eight Clubmobiles, a Cinemobile (a mini-movie theater on wheels which operated quite independently from the rest of us), two supply trucks, four English Hillmans, and

two jeeps—all painted a Red Cross gray. A sudden thought—
someone shouted, "Why don't we have Red Crosses on top of
our vehicles? We're non-combatants."

"Yeh, but we're not medics."

"Oh, so they can shoot at us, but we can't shoot back. Hah.
Hah."

Slowly, our caravan made its way to Southampton, and pulled
into the Staging Area just in time for the evening meal. The mess
hall was already filling up. After dinner, we had a baseball game
of sorts in an empty lot behind the barracks: a team of our girls
against the GI's. Afterwards, some of us went and sat in the grass
and sang in barbershop fashion, the old favored pastime of our
days overseas; much more my cup of tea than baseball. And as I
lay down on my cot that night, I heard some smothered giggles
at one end of the barracks and an argument at the other. How
our patterns of behavior stay with us, I thought. Now if they'd
just play taps, it might be a summer camp. Very soon, though, a
different type of experience summoned us. Hardly had we fallen
asleep, when a flashlight came roving through the barracks.
"Group H. On your feet. We're going."

With dawn breaking, the convoy of Clubmobiles started
slowly down the road with lights out, never getting out of second
gear during the short distance to the dock. Straining our eyes to
keep the truck ahead of us in sight, we eventually rolled down
the ramp to the sight of one of the now famous Liberty ships
awaiting us. Already, some other miscellaneous outfits of the
Army were waiting on the dock and we joined them as soon as
we got our trucks parked.

We sat on the dock for a K ration breakfast, over which we
talked to some of our fellow passengers, and then we took out
our bed rolls and stretched them out on the concrete floor of the
dock. The excitement had gradually oozed out with the daylight;
we were tired from lack of sleep, and the loading process was
obviously going to be a long wait. I didn't get much sleep, however,
because every time I opened one eye I caught sight of a male
uniform walking around looking us over. I don't sleep too well

with anyone watching me, but I knew if I sat up I would have an unwanted companion immediately and get no sleep at all.

Our Clubmobiles proved to be bulky problems when it came to hoisting them on board. Huge nets were wrapped around the trucks by a machine, a slow process after which a crane picked them up, carried them to the ship and then slowly, carefully, lowered them into the hold.

Finally, after about eight hours, on August 11, 1944, our vehicles were loaded, we scrambled on board and got fed. We unrolled our bedrolls on the deck and slept a wonderful, deep, sleep under the stars. The next day we awoke on the far side of the Channel in view of Utah Beach.

The first sight was of wrecked hulls of ships towed to the sides, but still sticking out of the water at frightful angles. We knew it had been cleaned up some since that day two months earlier, so could only imagine how much worse the reality was. Today it's strange to recall how different it was to digest the news. In that two months we had heard a lot about it and had seen news items, but we had no TV crews to take pictures of these shattering events and bring them to you in their immediacy. I am not sure if we knew the number of men who had been killed there that day—eight thousand graves now commemorate the American dead on a hill in Normandy—but we were aware it had to be a gruesome bloodbath. We did not know that it would be a sight shown over and over again in our lifetimes. At the time one could only look silently at the scene and wonder how those young men could bring themselves to do what they had obviously done. And wonder how any of them had survived. But as we stared, we knew the ones that had, plus many reinforcements, were rolling across the Continent. And we were out to catch up with them.

Unloading the Clubmobiles presented an even greater problem than loading them. The sea was rough, so lowering the vehicles onto the waiting barge was not going to be easy. The Captain of the ship explained to us that we would have to wait for calm water; otherwise a Clubmobile might meet a barge on the top of a wave with disastrous results. To avoid this calamity, we waited for six days, six impatient days of pinochle playing, picture taking, sleeping, eating and talking, with only one scare of an air raid.

In those six days, I became a fast friend of the radio operator on the ship—part of the merchant marine crew. It was wonderfully strange how speedily one could become buddies when you knew it would be short-lived. In breakneck speed, Dick, the radio operator, and I became close pals. Waiting out those six days to set foot on the Continent, the two of us propped ourselves against the side of the ship where it was shady, and had long, whole-hearted conversations about all the problems of the world. A strong bond of understanding grew between us, and we spoke to each other the way earnest young people of every generation do, with certainty that they can fix the world if only they would be called upon to do so.

Even if we had been inclined, there was little chance for romance, which in a way was a plus. Ours became an entrancing venture into the private world of the other gender with no sexual involvement, something as scarce as real treasure. Sitting on the ship for that many days at the site of the battle that had been a graveyard for so many it seemed natural to explore what we thought about the really "big questions." Most importantly It developed that both of us had families' where religion had been an on-again off-again thing.

In my teen age days my home was the scene of real discussions about religion, which I imagine is a rarity in most homes the world over. Undoubtedly most people grow up learning their religious thought along with the multiplication tables and accepting it with the same compliance. I believe that I was fortunate to have my parents disagree politely (well, almost) on the subject. My mother was a Christian Scientist which demands a leap of logic in defiance of empirical evidence which my father refused, and so we had, not arguments, but debates, over the question. I say this was fortunate because it developed in me a healthy skepticism, as well as an awareness that one's certainties can crumble without shaking the depths of one's world. Sitting there on the shipboard, I thought back to the days of those exhilarating discussions around the dinner table with my father's questions leading me way over my depth. And how certain I was of how I felt: at one time I could argue a good case for my mother's religion. But when I took Philosophy in college I realized the view was actually built upon a single fallacious syllogism, and worse yet, the syllogism was based on the unexamined premise that man was made in the image of God. Since it didn't seem to me that it was remotely possible that man was very God-like, no matter how much he thought he was, I felt compelled to discard the whole concept. However, rather than depressing me completely, it made me feel rather liberated, welcome to find my own way. And it was exciting to have a companion with a somewhat similar experience, which led him to agree with me that the really awesome thing is to comprehend how reality must exceed our capacity to understand it. The incomprehensible complexity of things we take for granted like the relationship between music and mathematics cannot be encompassed in a simple metaphysics. And this does not seem pessimistic to me. Rather, the wonder of it all keeps one's curiosity and interest alive, or at least it should.

I recall vividly sitting there with our knees up looking out at the sea. I can still see in front of me the rail framing the water as we thought those long thoughts, and how I was wondering if I would always feel that way. And I can say with assurance after all these years that I am more than ever impressed with the importance of trying to look with a clear eye. To keep searching for more understanding rather than certainty. To believe that which we want to be true because it is comforting seems to me a deadly error. The truth cannot always be comforting. But, no matter what, it is always interesting, and thought provoking.

At the end of the sixth day, the Captain finally decided that the sea was calm enough to entrust the precious donut machines to the hazards of the unloading process. It meant that we would have to spend the night on the barge since we couldn't land in the dark, but we were so elated at the prospect of getting off that we voted for it immediately and unanimously. Evening found us in full dress with helmet, musette bag, shoulder bag and canteen belt, climbing down the tricky rope ladder banging against the side of the ship onto the tops of the trucks, and finally giving the barge the shove off, heading for the shore. The sun was just setting as we came to a halt a few hundred yards from the beach. It would take daylight to prepare the ramp for our vehicles to take us to shore, so we curled up in the seat or on top of our luggage in the back. Some of us just sat up all night. About daybreak I became very hungry, and the smell of coffee lured me over to the little tugboat next to us. Here was a kitchen with some crusty provisions and two GI's looking like Tugboat Annie's crew who offered me some beans and C rations cooking on the stove with a "you're late" attitude.

Doris, Jean and I decided to settle the weighty question of who would get to drive the truck onto the beach by drawing straws, and Jean won. She excitedly bounced up and down in the driver's seat as we crossed the ramp onto the hard sand. Following the directions of waving M. P.'s we rolled up over a bank and onto an open road. As we emerged on the road, Jean bounced even more vigorously, saying, "Let's just keep driving and strike out for ourselves, shall we, shall we?" Doris and I nodded eagerly, knowing full well we would follow the wave of the next M. P.

As we did so, we followed a narrow, rutty road to a camp of sorts. Tents flapped in the breeze and some fires smoldered, left from the groups that had been there before us. As soon as those who'd missed the tugboat meal gulped down some K rations, we lined up and started off, following Eva up narrow dirt roads, almost falling out of our cabs in our eagerness to see the surroundings. It was the first time for all three of us to be on the Continent, (and in fact for almost everyone in the group, since traveling was limited to a lucky few during The Depression,) so we did not try to pretend to any nonchalance, happily giggling with excitement when a French woman almost fell over her chickens fluttering around her with surprise at seeing us. The three of us remarked naively that the backyards seemed to take the place of front yards, for there were always vegetables growing in the front of the gray stone houses. Of course we soon realized that after several years of occupation, it was quite understandable that everyone grew whatever was edible in all available soil.

We drove past an Army camp just outside of Cherbourg, the port on the English Channel northwest of Utah Beach, ending up in an apple orchard where we parked our Clubmobiles and gathered in a group to hear from Camilla, the head of the Clubmobile group in Europe. She had been one of the original Clubmobilers when they first started in England. She gave us our orders in a pleasant but firm, and authoritative voice.

We were to stay at the camp we had just passed for a few days (it was for transients like us) until final arrangements could be made. There were some more regulations about meals and other trivia.

And then, "You are to be attached to the XXth Corps," she said. "This is part of General Patton's Third Army, and you will serve whatever divisions and outfits are in that Corps. At the present time, there are the Seventh Armored and the Fifth Division . . . ."

I didn't hear anything beyond that. The Fifth Division, my division. I shouted with joy. but was quickly and definitely drowned out by the great groan that went up when she'd finished.

"What about the Second Armored Division?" several shouted at once. "We were promised we would be with that division."

"I'm sorry," Camilla said. "It is not in the Corps right now, but the Corps changes, and maybe later it will come into the XXth Corps. Anyway, you can't all be attached to one division."

Again I wished for Jane. It developed there **was** one other girl who had been in Ireland with the Fifth, but only for a week, so she hadn't had time to develop the attachment I harbored. Jean had transferred from Clubs to Clubmobile so that she could stay with the Second Armored, and was naturally disappointed. Doris was indifferent; she had been with a completely different division in England so didn't know whether to rejoice with me or commiserate with Jean.

Except for me, it was a rather dejected group going about the

business of finding a tent and putting up cots. Chance was with me
for once, and I couldn't help showing my glee. Being the only one in
such high spirits did not endear me to the rest of the group, so I did
my best to stifle it somewhat, not too successfully. The collective
spirit visibly rose, however, when we were told that we would be
allowed to take turns going into Cherbourg in the little Hillmans.

On our turn Jean, Doris and I drank in our first sight of a
French city; all gray stone relieved only by chocolate brown signs,
embroidered with gold lettering such as "Patisserie,"
"Confectionerie." We heard that a Red Cross club was already
established there, and we considered it our ordained duty to make
it our first stop. We found it easily by the big American flag, and
went in the small stone building, changed dollars into "invasion
francs," and had a cup of coffee along with the GI's. I remember
standing in line, exchanging the usual banter with the guys,
knowing this was a moment I'd remember the rest of my life,
the combination of all my senses alive at the same instant. The
odor, the peculiar odor of France, which I found rather pleasant
though penetrating; the shuffling of GI Boots, the weight of the
ridiculously heavy handbag on my shoulder, the American flags
along with numerous division emblems tacked on the battleship
gray walls, and the sounds of the GI voices battling each other to
be heard over the heavy laughter.

This is Cherbourg, I kept telling myself. This is France, the
Continent. You are here. You are here! I looked down at my dirty
cuffs sticking out from the sleeves of my uniform and felt the
contrast to that preconceived picture I'd fashioned of a war heroine
from all those books about the first World War, when I had seen
myself as sort of a wraith with a red cross emblazoned on some
white flowing robes, spreading protecting wings over suffering
humanity. But, Hemingway not withstanding, I was no dream-
like wraith. I was a human being with dirty cuffs and a shiny
nose, entirely too conscious of both, standing in line with two
equally un-wraithlike coworkers, all of us full of the complexities
and foibles that make us human, and all of us most of the time
tongue-tied to the extent that anything we had to say would be

expressed in a few standard phrases of Army slang like "My Aching Back," or "That's S.O.P." (Standard Operating Practice—for when something goes wrong or is snafu.)

Withal, this was our first day in France. Jean and I weren't sure we could talk to a Frenchman, but Doris had taught French in civilian life, and I suspect after struggling for years to get her students to say "C'est la plume de ma tante," she could not quite believe that she wouldn't lapse into English when the going got tough. Holding a conversation with anyone but Americans always made us feel as if we were playing hooky, but that day we slipped away from all Americans and into a French cafe with great abandon. Fortunately, it was full of French men and we had to sit with other people. They were obviously pleased to see us and motioned to us to sit down.

To answer their questions, Jean and I practiced our "Je suis avec le Croix Rouge," and then Doris took over, actually striking up a conversation. Gradually, when she realized they understood her, her cheeks got as red as her flaming hair.

"That was fun," she said as we walked out the door to go back to base.

"Fun? Bless me," I thought. "That was as exciting as a first kiss."

"Somewhere in France."

TEN

O ur goal—the XXth Corps of Patton's Third Army— was racing across France with unlikely speed. We knew it would be hard for us to catch up with them and this made us even more anxious to get started, but we had to wait once again for two days in an almost continuous rain, while Eva, with the help of her newly appointed co-supervisor Angela, got the necessary data together. Finally we pumped up all the flat tires with our bicycle pumps and set out from an apple orchard just south of Cherbourg: a convoy of eight Clubmobiles, the Cinemobile, four Hillmans and two jeeps. Out on the road starting east over the north of France, our frustration disappeared with the sunshine.

For three weeks, our convoy lumbered across France, traveling the same distance that our supply trucks would later do in two days. Sometimes it seemed that we would get there faster if we got out and walked, but this was not the Red Ball Highway, and we were a convoy. Wincing for the donut machines at every jolt, we had to go slowly, and when one vehicle had to stop we all had to stop. Consequently, at the end of the day, when we felt we should have crossed the entire continent, we'd discover that we'd barely covered eighty to one hundred miles.

The French were still in their first flush of loving Americans for liberating them, and we American women were a new and unexpected sight to them. In every town as we trundled into view they hung out the windows over the narrow streets shouting

"Femmes! Femmes Americaines!" Since we were going so slowly, we carried on brief conversations through the windows; Jean and I with our halting French playing accompaniment to Doris with her more fluent command.

When we stopped, they swarmed over us, wanting to know what we were and the intent of our mission. Even Doris couldn't come up with a word for "donuts" in French, so we settled on the word for cakes. We showed them our Clubmobiles and tried to explain, to their inevitable mystification, that we would make "gateaux" in the machines and feed them to our troops. It was obvious that they didn't know what to make of us, and at first we thought they may have put us down as a luxurious auxiliary to the kitchen crews.

Stopping for a half-hour that first day in a small village, the three of us from the "Cedar Rapids" went window shopping and met a plump, pleasant looking girl who jumped off her bicycle and accosted us with great enthusiasm.

"You are Americans?" she said. "How nice. At last I shall have an opportunity to tell someone how much we appreciate what you have accomplished for us. I see all these American men come through here but It is necessary that I do not talk to them, you understand."

"Why not?" We hadn't noticed any such hesitancy.

"Lots of our girls do, I know. But I am a school teacher. I teach English," she said shyly. "And, well, I am not accustomed to speaking to strange young men. It is hard? No? Actually, I am not accustomed to speaking to any young men. I am twenty three, but I was eighteen when all of the young men in our village were taken, and I have seen none during these important years."

We felt a great responsibility at representing America and being the recipients of such sincere gratitude. We also felt compassion for her plight, but we could think of nothing better to do than to allow her to pick out the brand of perfume we should buy. Itseemed to give her some small feeling of reciprocity.

I don't suppose any Americans went across France with quite the mixed emotions we had. The GI's could take it as their just due, even if they were never to see action of any kind, but sometimes we felt a little ashamed at reaping the harvest someone else had sown. Even if we didn't stop, going through the little towns, local residents thrust all kinds of presents into our hands as we went by: champagne, medals, souvenirs, wooden shoes, anything they thought we might cherish. And when we did stop, they hurried off to their homes, bidding us wait until they came back with more. Being human, we enjoyed feeling like conquering heroines, sometimes so much so we had to laugh at ourselves.

One time, for instance, we came to a small town in Eastern Normandy to find the square lined with a huge crowd. Whether the lead car really missed the turn I'll never know, but we went around the square twice, bowing and waving like a squad of royal princesses. Minutes later, when we stopped, we learned that the crowd was waiting for De Gaulle who had become the hero of France after the invasion turned the tide. He was to make a speech there. We hastened on our way.

The drenching rain came back again and after several days of searching for suitable places to bivouac each night and some dismal failures with collapsing pup tents, everything we had was soaked through so we felt we had to take time to dry ourselves out. We found a Special Services Company that was also attached to the XXth Corps and established ourselves in the field next to them, arranging our vehicles in a line next to a large protective hedgerow. The sun came out in full force, and we spread our soggy belongings along the tops of the Clubmobiles and washed our hair for the first time since England in the allotted two helmets-full of water. Then we laid ourselves out to dry wherever we could find a sunny spot.

In the supply truck, we found a couple of pyramidal tents, which we had never attempted to put up because no one knew how. However, upon request, a squad from the Special Services Unit came marching over and directed us—and I do mean directed—in the proper procedure for pitching these large tents. When they were in place, we also got a lesson in digging latrines and pitching latrine flaps and these latter skills (unlike the pitching of the huge tent) proved to be invaluable in our career overseas. At the end of this bit of sharpening, we set up our wooden cots and were quite comfortable for a day or two. The sun obligingly stayed with us and I retain a vision of us standing expectantly (yes, expectantly) in the chow line with our mess kits to get some C rations. The C rations might have looked like canned dog food but they were at least heated and a step up from the K rations which we had been living on: that notorious package of nutritious (but not delicious) crackers accompanied by a can of Spam or similar cold meat or cheese.

Some of the girls even rigged up a shower, consisting of a flap between two Clubmobiles. One person went in to the space between the flaps and undressed, while someone else readied a bucket of water that'd been heated on the field ranges in the huge coffee cauldron to dump over her. In a couple of hours, there was enough hot water for two very brief showers.

I was standing talking to "Texas" a long-legged strawberry blonde from Austin. We were both in our bathing suits waiting our turn for the shower, looking disconsolately at each other.

"You know, it will be hours before it gets to us. Anyway, I'd much rather go swimming. There must be some place around here. Didn't we pass a stream not far from here?" Always anxious to get in the water, I look at her hopefully.

Jack, our one and only GI, overhearing our conversation, quickly joins us. It flashes through my head that Jack is usually there when I needed him. How convenient, I think. And how come? Or am I imagining it?

"Yeah. I heard from these guys that they found a neat little swimming pool. It's just up over that hill I think." He points up the little road that had brought us here.

The three of us climb into the Hillman and are off in a flash to find the rumored spot the GI's had claimed. We wend our way up the narrow road past the hedgerow out into the bright sunshine, passing two fertile fields of vines laden with grapes. Gradually we hear the voices of Americans having fun. Turning off the narrow road to an even smaller one we follow the source up a slight incline onto a little bridge. Some French women are standing there looking down on the stream at the noisy bathers below. We stop and suddenly the pleasant little scene turns into a minor bedlam. Never has our sign "American Red Cross" on the Hillman had more effect. We hear the shouts in the familiar accents of our countrymen.

"American women! American women!"

But these shouts are not of delight and expectancy but of consternation. The gleam of naked bodies scurrying for cover and the nonplused look on the French women's faces bring it all home at once. The Frenchwomen can't understand why the consternation. But we can. Jack, quickly turns us around to avoid our catching a glimpse, and drives back off the bridge. With our faces safely turned the other way, he gets out of the car to go back and make a deal, returning with this report "Give them a half-hour more, and then you can have the pool."

As we drove off to while away the time, I looked back to see the French women settling down comfortably on the rail again, undisturbed as if nothing had happened, leaving Texas and me amused but confused. Jack just shook his head.

The G I's were true to their word and we had the pool to ourselves for a wonderfully refreshing swim. We had brought along a bar of soap, too, and remarked longingly that there would have been an advantage to be without a bathing suit. After that swim and a rest back by the hedgerow, except for the sound of distant shelling, the K rations we had to resort to were almost as good as a picnic, complete to swarms of yellow jackets that always descended the moment we opened a can of cheese or meat, covering the food almost immediately. I remember them so well because I carelessly put one of the crackers in my mouth and bit through a yellow jacket. Naturally, it retaliated right on the tip of my tongue. Jack was at my side immediately when I gave a screech and showed so much concern I knew I had not imagined that he had formed a special regard for me.

This skinny-dipping incidence remained in my thoughts for some time. The humour of it was to be relished, but there was another side of it that made me wonder. I was struck with how our taken-for-granted Puritan background made for this big difference in how we Americans looked at the situation and how the French viewed it. But even more, how the GI's were so disturbed by the American woman's presence but not the French. When in Rome? I would be confronted with this puzzling question more than once in the coming months.

And too, I would be reminded of the different attitudes of our cultures again and again. When we came to Epernay some time later, one of our girls tried to get a room for a GI who had been separated from his outfit. She was told, with no hesitation, "Well, of course, he can share your room." Soon everyone knew about this incident—a complete and unexpected shocker to us. How surprised we would have been had we known that sharing rooms would be the accepted state of affairs in the United States fifty years later.

I came out of college with the conviction gleaned from sociology classes that it was wrong ("politically incorrect" came later) to generalize about people by nationality. Human beings constitute one species and are all fundamentally the same. That was the "correct" attitude. And one I bought into with great confidence.

And yet. Here I was seeing undeniable and distinct national differences. Besides, it had become the accepted picture to categorize our enemy as nefarious, depraved and evil; in complete contradiction of my conviction that "all people are brothers." Trying to harmonize these two conflicting concepts occupied my thoughts at a time in my life when it seemed I must make all these decisions for myself, since there was so much confusion in the thoughts of others.

I often thought back to "All Quiet on the Western Front," the poignant story of a young German soldier in the first World War who might as well have been a young American soldier. The same feelings, the same conscience. In the end he is needlessly killed by a stray bullet and you are made to feel just as sorry for him as you would for an American. Like many other people, when I read this as a young girl I was strongly convinced that all killing in war is essentially needless and wrong. Yet here we were again fighting the same people with no doubts as to the legitimacy of the war. Indubitably, the distinctive character of WW II was the almost unanimous justification we felt in fighting it and the certainty we felt that we were doing the right and moral thing. Except for some conscientious objectors, (who were unfortunately mostly treated like prisoners) there were none of the protests that have marked the conflicts we have stumbled into ever since. The attack on Pearl Harbor had effectively made self-defense the strong justification.

ELEVEN

By mid-August, following the trail of the Third Army, so well-blazed with crumbling stone and gaping houses, we had caught up with some of the the troops in the rear of those pushing their way through France so quickly. We still kidded about the war being over before we could catch up with them, but sometimes when we stopped for a breathing spell, we squeezed in a batch or two of donuts for some stray units: a Post Office Unit or Special Services detached from a division. Maybe one hundred men temporarily housed in an old crumbling building or a campsite, anywhere they could set up for business.

But there were only two or three donut machines that had withstood the journey intact, and we discovered the time and effort it took to start the field ranges to heat enough water for even fifty cups of coffee was incredible. Each donut and coffee we served up at this point came at the expense of a grueling experience of unloading and reloading, making for frazzled tempers. The unwieldy benches that were part of our supplies and which had to be lifted out for serving and put back in afterwards seemed a particularly unnecessary back-breaker. We never ran into anyone too short to reach the counter without it, so one by one they all became left behind during this period, not inadvertently. We didn't run into any more great rain storms so we seldom even put up our pup tents, let alone the pyramidal ones. It was much easier to flop down on the ground with our sleeping bags. Exhaustion is a good soporific.

At long last, during the early part of September, we rolled into a charming little town, in the heart of the Champagne district—the Marne country east of Paris. (We bypassed Paris, unfortunately missing the big celebration of the city's liberation.) The many little houses dotting the narrow streets of this village, Epernay, were all neat and trim with picturesque flowers hanging from their balconies. Their appearance seemed to speak of their owners defiance by keeping up spirits through those agonizing war years. When we stopped near a little hotel, Eva informed us that due to a gas shortage, the forward troops—the honest to goodness fighting Army, the Fifth Division in fact—was stalled nearby, and tomorrow we would begin to do the actual job we were there to do. Not only that, but we could leave our Clubmobiles in the square and give up our bed rolls on the ground for a stay in this hotel for two nights. Suddenly thirty-one tired and dirty girls were bounding around with renewed enthusiasm and vigor expressing great appreciation for this appealing little inn, with flowers hanging everywhere you looked. The beds were a definite improvement over the ground, and though the water was miserly, running into small sinks instead of bathtubs, the champagne made up for it. It never stopped flowing.

In order to start serving the next day, donuts would have to be made through the night. Six months later we would have taken a dim view of such a prospect, but now we were more than eager. We drew lots to see who would bake and who would serve. The "Cedar Rapids" was to bake.

One scene that night stands out clearly in my memory. I stepped outside to get another pail of water, and the moonlit night was such a relief from the hot and smoky truck that I stood there for a moment, pail in hand, reluctant to go back in. We had moved the Clubmobiles to a lonely field, and in the moonlight they made a weirdly beautiful picture. The back door of the Clubmobile had to be dropped because of the blackout (all across France the blackout was permanent as camouflage from German planes) so only a tiny shaft of light showed where the electric cord trailed out. Huddled together in this lonely field, the Clubmobiles looked like four friendly monsters, each with its umbilical cord stretched to the generator. The loud hum of the generator reverberated in the silence, punctuated by the sounds of war from afar. It seemed impossible that such an innocent process as making donuts could be going on inside.

When I went back in, there was Jean, sitting placidly on an empty flour barrel, spearing the donuts as they came around. We had to change our usual routine in order to transport them to the other Clubmobiles more easily, so we put them into one of the empty barrels rather than the regular trays. This was the first time either of us had done it in this way, which was unfortunate as I was to learn later. We worked through most of the night until the next shift came on, and then gratefully took over the beds in the hotel as they were deserted. I did not get the full benefit of that bed, though, because I couldn't bear the thought of not being on hand to serve the Fifth, my division. I knew I had no right to ask anyone to trade jobs with me, but I thought that no one could object if I just went along with those scheduled to serve and Eva agreed. So after a few hours' sleep, I joined the "Topeka" crew as the fourth Red Cross girl on their Clubmobile, and came to feel very much a fifth wheel.

Our guides led us through Verdun and into another orchard where the first outfit was supposed to be. We waited for some time, my excitement keeping me awake. Eventually the troops came straggling in, but to my great disappointment they were from the other half of the division, the one I didn't know, which had been around Newcastle in Ireland. We found two other outfits among the trees, but again I didn't know any of them.

To make things worse, much worse, we were serving the donuts that Jean and I had made the night before, and the crew of the Clubmobile knew it. We had layered them the usual way, one row on top of another but it soon became apparent that putting hot donuts in barrels takes an amount of finesse that neither Jean nor I possessed. When we got about half-way through the barrel, instead of nice crusty round things, the donuts were mashed, and crumbly and finally just sodden parts. Tired and depressed, I retired to a corner to indulge in a bit of self-flagellation ably assisted by the remarks of the other three girls who had to serve those donuts. I must admit they looked as if they had been hurled helter-skelter from a distance, and there was little I could say in our defense.

One of the guides that day insisted on driving (that never happened on my Clubmobile), so two of the girls of the crew rode up front with him and the third one rode in the back with me and the second guide. Riding in the back, bracing yourself against a counter with no air and all the utensils banging around your heads as the Clubmobile rolled from side to side, was never fun. This day was worse than usual for it was all we could do to keep on our feet. In my depressed mood, I was just as glad that conversation was impossible with the sound of distant firing outside competed with the banging inside.

Suddenly, the truck came to an abrupt halt and the sharp staccato of rapid-fire bullets sounded very close indeed. Our guides were as green as we were, but we'd been informed and warned about strafing, "Leave your vehicles and spread so the target will not be concentrated." Our guide was closest to the door, so he quickly opened the little door in the bottom half of the divided back door and crawled through the small opening. I was close after him, and as I started to crawl through, he turned back towards me and I caught an expression on this lad's face that I shall never forget—two emotions so visibly competing for supremacy. Should he run for safety, or must he help us out? Save his own life or help a woman from a car? I gave him a push, which freed him, and he was off like a deer. I was laughing inside so hard as I rolled into a ditch that I almost forgot to be scared. As it was, the plane passed quickly overhead aiming for bigger and better targets so we picked ourselves up off the ground in a few minutes and came back feeling very relieved.

I'm sure that the next few weeks are the ones Clubmobile girls think of when we say, "I was in the ETO." We were still full of vigor and enthusiasm and so were the men we served. Those who had been in combat were thankful for being alive, and as yet the complete apathy that eventually overtook them had not appeared. During this time we were very much on our own, as the Army was too busy moving forward to worry much about us. The XXth Corps knew we existed, but they paid little attention to us for seven weeks. Then when they realized that we were up close to the fighting front, we got the terse order. "Get the hell, back and quick." We were told that we were not to be exposed to danger needlessly because it cost too much to get us there and we were not expendable. (Eva, with a sardonic twinkle in her eye, suggested it might be that Corps Forward was a bit chagrined at having women ahead of them.)

In any event, for these seven weeks, we operated as best we could without interference or concern from anyone. We leeched on to any outfit that was available and convenient. These were the supporting groups: the Medical, the T.D (tank destroyers) and the like, behind the front lines of the rifle infantry divisions. We could share their quarters-tents, Nissen huts or stark buildings commandeered by the Army—and their chow, going out from there to serve the fighting infantry when they were pulled back for a break. We were never made to feel like unwelcome parasites. In fact, it was a thrill to be welcomed with whoops of delight when these outfits discovered we were to be attached to them. And even more of a thrill to be welcomed by the ones we went out to serve on their well-deserved pull-back periods, especially if it were their first time to see us. In the face of some of the criticism confronted upon coming home and even still today: sarcastic remarks like "I never even saw a Red Cross girl" or "they were only for the officers," I can always bring to mind the glad tidings at our arrival.

"Hey, there you are. Why weren't you on the beach to greet us when we landed?" Or: "I'd walk a mile for a donut and a smile. I just did."

And they often had, when we could get no closer to them. I remind myself, when listening to these disparaging remarks, that so many of those we served are no longer with us because we concentrated on the infantry as we should have because they are the ones who really did the fighting.

The men were still full of themselves, not yet so lethargic, struggling to keep up the bravado. Sometimes the coffee and donuts were attacked with a fervor appropriate for manna from heaven when the straggling line came back a few at a time from a dug-in position in fox holes where they'd had no hot coffee for days. Unfortunately, just at those times when we needed them most, we would sometimes run out of our wares. Two donuts each and one canteen of coffee for a company of forty or fifty men was all we could manage to make, but men's fists could close on four or five donuts from our trays on the counter.

"Hey, chow hounds," we'd yell. "Think of your buddies. There won't be enough to go around." Or: "Have all you want. Have two. Do you hear me?" But our words usually went unheeded, and we hated to seem stingy.

After our two nights in Epernay, we had moved up to what we called "Medic Hill," the Medical Corps of the Fifth Division situated not far from Epernay on a hill overlooking the main road going east. Naturally, it seemed, this unit was not the one I had known in Ireland. The Special Services Sergeant for the division, who was our main liaison, was someone I'd not seen before either. He soon got to know me, though, because I became the little gadfly, trailing after him, begging for news of "my half of the Division" and when we could serve them.

This was at the time of the eventful gas shortage, when the troops were stalled for weeks, but they finally mobilized again and we watched convoy after convoy come rolling by, starting back into combat. One morning as we were making our donuts I looked out the window of the Clubmobile and saw the markings of the Fifth Division on the bumpers of the trucks in this convoy. I threw down the dough, wiping my hands on my apron, and jumped down to the ground to dash down the hill, stumbling in the weeds and ruts. When I got to the road, I saw that sure enough it was my regiment, my battalions, even Company I riding in those trucks. I recognized some of the men hanging on the vehicles and some recognized me. I must have looked a little silly standing there by myself jumping up and down, but I continued doing so until the last truck had rolled by. I knew they must be headed for combat, but that they would be brought back to camps around the area when not fighting. And so it was that gradually I saw here and there a few of the outfits I had known in Ireland, when they could be brought back from the front. It was very rewarding to be recognized and to see some familiar faces. I believe the Red Cross hadn't wanted us to get too attached to any one outfit. That's why they moved most everybody around a lot. But there is no denying that the long stay in Ireland, with its bonding, brought an added fillip to the contacts.

And then one day I learned that Company I was pulled back on rest in the vicinity not far from Medic Hill, although not yet fitted into our schedule. The liaison officer told me where they were—about two kilometers away—bedded down in a thicket. It would not be hard to get there, and they would be glad to furnish a guide.

I persuaded Eva to let me make an unscheduled trip. She agreed without resistance, but insisted I take someone with me, so I asked Dee, the captain of another crew, who had become someone I would turn to. She agreed as I knew she would, and we loaded up one of the smaller trucks with donuts and coffee urns and followed our guide down a little cow-path of a road.

It was a pleasant day in September with the sun bright and low in the heavens. The still-green leaves cast merry shadows around us belying the distant roll of shelling as we drove deeper and deeper into the woods and finally halted at signs of a camp. Abruptly, my excitement took a different turn. It was like coming to a reunion where you're pretty sure of a welcome, but a buried element of doubt peeks out. Maybe, just maybe, you've over estimated the bond. Perhaps they won't be as happy to see you as you think. I waited anxiously as we honked the horn. One by one, the men drifted out from their tents so well hidden behind the trees.

"Well, bless me. If I'd knowed you was comin' I'd a baked a cake."

Beautiful, lovely words. There was no reception committee, because they didn't know we were coming, but this was more fun. There were some new faces replacing familiar ones, but as yet their casualties had not been great. (They were not part of the actual D Day beach invasion.) I ran over to the kitchen flap, and there were Joe and Mike working over the same old infernal field range.

"Well, look who's here."

They roused the rest of the kitchen crew from their siestas, and we had our picture taken first thing, with Mike holding up the bottle of whiskey that they had been saving in my honor. I can't stand whiskey straight, but I would have drunk out of this "loving bottle" if it had been castor oil. American whisky was hard for GI's to come by over there, and this gesture was more than heart-warming; it brought tears to my eyes. I felt all my fierce loyalty was vindicated that day. This bond with a whole bunch of guys who could tease me like a little sister may have been nothing like the role I had pictured in my imagination, but it was just as satisfying at that moment.

Obviously the camaraderie among the GI's who had been in combat had taken on another facet, too. Their new togetherness forged in the dependence of combat was evident. I became aware that even their feelings toward their officers, which had sometimes been voiced in menacing threats about what would happen in combat when the officer was in front of them, changed when their lives depended on his leadership. They talked in quite different tones especially about the one captain they had often bitterly envisioned with a bullet in his back, when they were especially disgruntled.

When we left this spot I thanked Dee for coming with me and in her warm and empathetic way she squeezed my arm and said, "It made me very happy for you. It was great." I knew I had made a friend for life.

In the middle of September we packed up our tents at Medic Hill, and moved inside into a nearby monastery with an A.P.O. (American Post Office) unit. We were elated to give up sleeping on the ground, but we still had to dig a latrine. Our part of the monastery was just a huge, completely barren room, with a concrete flight of stairs. When we climbed these stairs to a latrine we laughed and appointed the usual detail to start digging. Hardly worthwhile climbing steps to get to this one: a simple concrete floor sloping down to a hole in the center with two raised blocks for your feet. It must have been connected with plumbing, but I hope it worked better for the monks. When we were there, you pulled a chain, and then a faint, very faint trickle of water wended its way between your feet. Better the fresh outdoors.

The courtyard of the monastery made an excellent place to park our Clubmobiles and cook our donuts. We cooked one day, served the next and had one day a week off. While we were there, we also had to take turns serving as a kitchen crew. The Army was supposed to feed us wherever we went and could draw extra rations for us, but this post office unit seemed to be somewhat of an orphan with few rations and no cooks. We took their few rations and supplemented them with what we could find, scouring the countryside, barter in hand. We didn't need much French to walk up to a man or woman bending over a hoe in a field and hold out cigarettes, to get potatoes or eggs or whatever in return. (We figured the cigarettes we gave out freely to the troops were legitimate barter material for our sustenance.) Then we would come back with our potatoes and onions, or whatnot and see if we could outdo the last cooks in making rations unrecognizable. There was one girl of Hungarian descent, Zimmy, who suddenly acquired the stature of Authority on the subject. With a foresight we all envied, she had brought along her own supply of spices and herbs. She taught us that Hungarian goulash is justly famous, for it can be made from almost anything with the right seasonings, especially Hungarian paprika, which is in a class of its own.

For a week or so, it was almost exhilarating to do our own cooking, always with an eye to outdoing the last crew. However, before long, fatigue dictated that we lose interest in this experience.

Days later, we moved just a few miles to a chateau in Jarny that had been taken over by a T. D. group. This chateau, viewed from the outside, was a veritable mansion. Indeed, we felt a little guilty as we drove our trucks down into the lower grounds to park them. It was ideal from a practical point of view. There was a big circular courtyard to give us room to maneuver and a road leading around the chateau to a large, grassy field, where we could keep our Clubmobiles when making donuts. But, as we stood down there and looked up at the chateau, with its beautifully landscaped lawns rising away from a romantic little pond, it seemed made for better things than heavy boots and dual tires. One could imagine a pompadoured Madame with her chevalier whisking around the trees. But already a baseball game had begun.

Inside, however, the chateau was not quite so sumptuous. Germans had obviously been there before us, for all the furniture had been removed and what was left of the family—a woman and her son—seemed quite accustomed to living in a small wing of the house. Actually, I suppose the chateau may have had an elegance we overlooked because of the most obtrusive fact that it had no bathroom. What a disappointment that was. We could not fathom that the rather dilapidated outhouse could be the only substitute for our all too familiar latrines.

This preoccupation with latrines may seem rather ignoble to anyone left from my generation, or perhaps it may seem a misguided effort to keep up with the modern world where the bathroom is the preordained seat of comedy. Still, for us it was a very real concern. As anyone who has ever ridden in one of those old GMC 6x6 knows, they are not noted for their comfort in normal circumstances, given plenty of gas stations, but in our world, void of all ladies' rooms, they became instruments of torture, particularly on the long ride home as the three of us bounced up and down with agonized faces, unable to converse, unable to think.

The woods, the lonely protective woods beckoned to us, but like a restraining hand, the inevitable sign loomed up in front. "Mines Cleared to Hedges." It became a standard refrain. "Mines Cleared to Hedges. Mines Cleared to Hedges." Once Jean stopped the truck in her impulsive and final manner and started for the hedges.

"Blown up one way or another, what does it matter?" she shrugged.

We restrained her only by force. A car did not pass us on that road for the next few minutes, and I'm quite sure we should not have cared if one had.

At first, in our naivete, when it became necessary, we would inquire of the outfit we were serving, in our best matter-of-fact tone, where the latrine was. We had commented often enough on the fact that evidently the French thought that women were above the mundane need to go, because while there were plenty of urinals for men, even in the villages, there was nothing at all for women. But we didn't expect the same belief from our fellow nationals; thus, blithely, we asked, "Where's the latrine?" We were dismayed to find that with few exceptions, this particular question generated confusion bordering on panic.

We discovered why when a very red-in-the-face officer asked us to wait a few minutes, and then we walked into a latrine flap that was obviously still swaying from the last hammer stroke. Still, rephrasing our question to "Do you have a latrine?" did little to assuage the confusion. At first, it didn't make sense, considering that the Army was hardly distinguished for its prudery. After all, these were the men for whom a cartoon character had been named "Couchez Avec" (want to sleep with me?) supposedly illustrating the common GI greeting to French women. Why did they react so differently to us? It was another example of that reaction we had found with the GI's skinny-dipping comfortably in front of women until we came along. Why was that?

I came to believe that it was simply that an American woman speaking the same language stood for home. And home—Puritan America—was far, far removed from the present life of the Army. The prudery, so completely abandoned with the French women, came back forcibly whenever confronted with us. It was as if a long line of mothers, grandmothers and school teachers presented themselves, suddenly demanding why there was no latrine.

I felt this attitude was something basic, and later on became convinced of it. One of the girls wrote a short essay for "The Sinker" on latrines, entitling it "Flushless, Blushless, Flushless." It was an entertaining account of our tribulations in finding latrines and a description of the various species encountered. We thought it was hilariously funny and nothing remotely shocking so passed it on to some of our GI buddies. I was amazed to have several of these men tell me that they saw nothing funny in it, and were shocked that such a nice girl could write such an essay. I guess that girls like us, who reminded them of their girls back home, also reminded them that nice American women should be "above" such ribaldry. Evidently we were to dwell on an uncomfortable pedestal, dirty boots, pants and all. And once again, I bemoaned the subtle arrogance towards non-American women this attitude implied.

TWELVE

A s we knew it would, our stay at the Jarny chateau brought
on the mud. What was once a nice green field, upon
acquaintance with our trucks, became just a huge sea of slimy
mud. All it took was a spattering of rain because It never seemed
to dry out. With the same thing happening in all the fields we
stopped in, that whole section of northeastern France just
southwest of Luxembourg seemed to be built upon earth that
oozed. On the days we served, we came home with coffee urns
caked with mud. It was a nice little feat to wash them out and
keep them sanitary while standing in mud up over the soles of
your boots. On the days we cooked donuts, the last hour was
spent in shoveling, scraping and scrubbing the mud out of the
truck.

I can still see Doris in her stocking feet as she held the floor rag
distantly with two fingers as if it were a dead rat, and daintily stepped
over a passably clean floor, saying fervently "Therrr . . . . r." Then,
just as daintily, sliding out the back door, slipping her feet into her
muddy boots, which she treated like Cinderella's slippers. When
Jean and I did it we usually transferred most of the mud from the
floor onto ourselves, but Doris did everything carefully, stepping her
way through life like a sword dance.

It was here, too, that one of the T.D. group, whose I.Q. was
usually showing, felt he had found in our Doris his soul mate.
He'd have liked to spend the rest of his life, and he tried to spend

the rest of the war, admiring Doris at her work. Most of all, he liked to see her scrub the floor, for then he could say, "If you marry me, you won't have to get down on your knees. I'll buy you a mop with a handle." Doris laughed at this sally every time, which proves that red hair does not always entail quick tempers.

I'm afraid that we should have become stuck in the mud here forever, if we had not acquired four more GI's attached to us to help out. Up until this time, as I have said, we were operating with only one. Actually, we needed at least two electricians to keep our generators and donut machines in working order, and there were no electricians among the girls. Jack, our one GI, was the kind of person who could fix most anything, but he was more than delighted to get some help. Now, the trucks and field ranges could be maintained as they should be. Furthermore, it meant he could find some time to spend with me.

Somewhere along the line, I realized I was not imagining that Jack had his eyes set on me, and we became a twosome. He was, to me, a new and fascinating type of man: of Irish descent, from South Boston, with a decided New England accent. I have to admit I had harbored the stereotype that anything resembling a Harvard accent indicated superior learning and pomposity so it tickled me to hear him talking in the ordinary jargon of the GI with some of the usual mistakes of grammar, in this decided high-brow accent. His dark brown eyes, full of mischief and laughter, the kind that always appealed to me, and his almost-Roman nose belied his Irish descent.

One night he found me starting to read "How Green Was My Valley", a book that I had somehow acquired and from then on we read it together. He obviously had never really before experienced the delight of becoming involved in another world with someone else. A green valley became a sort of code word for anything he found delightful like a simple day off to be together and head for Luxembourg. It was great fun to introduce someone so appreciative to a new kind of experience, and it was soon very satisfying to have him waiting for me at the end of the serving day. I thought back to the girl in Ireland who had told us new girls that an ETO romance was inevitable, but no good could come from it. She was probably right, I thought, but the important thing about this romance was that we both from the beginning accepted the ephemeral nature of it.

Most everyone in that setting came to understand that the background of the war made a world so far removed from normality that the human craving for close relationships would find outlets intended for this milieu only. Naturally, there were some liaisons that became permanent. One of our group who got married that winter entered a marriage that lasted fifty years. But in most cases neither the past, nor thought of the future intruded. They—the past and the future—pertained in only an unclear way to this all-encompassing now. "Connection" or sometimes "connectedness" (maybe that sounds more personal?) is at present a favorite word. It's as if we've just discovered the primal urge to be attached intimately to people who care. Obviously it is part of our human nature and will in different ways in diverse environments find its path. In this distinctive setting of the war for me and for this "now", it was nice to have a special person to come home to. No matter where we were, Jack would have fixed up some corner, maybe just a tarp attached to one of the generators, with a coffee pot and some kind of little heater which would have "coziness" written all over it beckoning me at the end of the day.

Naturally, any of my letters home for some time had included accounts of "Jack and I did this or that." Later, near the end of the war when we knew it was coming, my sister wrote to me asking who this Jack was and why I was so non-communicative about him. Was it serious? In my answer to her I said, "As for Jack, he didn't rate a serious word, I guess, because I always knew it wasn't serious. We were always together so I couldn't help talking about him, but it is practically over. You see, he has a wife at home. I wonder if you can realize how little difference that makes over here. "

As I recently reread this letter I remember thinking at the time that it was probably impossible for anyone not there to understand. And I can still picture the time I discovered that he had a wife. It was not long after we had become a twosome and it was on a morning of my day off when we had made some kind of plans. He came by to pick me up and we began walking up a gravel path. We walked along in silence for some time except for the scuffling of the gravel. I knew there was something bothering him, and finally he stopped, lit a cigarette and turned to me, leaning his body against a tree for support.

"I have something to tell you," he said looking at me disconsolately.

"Yes?"

He took a long drag on his cigarette and let it out slowly, gaining time. In an instant, I surmised what he was going to say, although I had not thought of it before. But I let him struggle on.

"Well, you know, I feel bad about . . . well, deceiving you . . . I know I should have told you before but . . . . I never expected this, you know, I'm in love with you but I'm not really free. I have a wife at home. I'm sorry I didn't tell you."

"Mmm. Yes. They should make men wear wedding rings." (Double-ring marriages were not yet that commonplace). We walked on for a while, my thoughts centering on how I was not truly surprised and how insignificant it seemed, whereas before at home it would have been a bombshell. And how little difference it would make. And how marriage had never entered my mind. It was some minutes before I asked him a few questions about this marriage which he answered tersely.

And then breathlessly, he blurted out, "I haven't written to her for a long time, and I know it isn't fair to her but I can't tell her about us," he said.

"No, you can't, but you must write to her. She's probably worried to death."

"Well, she knows I'm not in any danger."

"Well, she can't really know, no matter what you tell her. Anyway, anybody might get killed over here and if she doesn't hear from you . . . . Please do write to her."

I took his silence for consent, and by the time we got in the jeep the need to discuss it further had disappeared. That it would make no difference in our present relationship was a tacit agreement sealed with the start of the motor.

One disadvantage with this liaison was that in the beginning I had little time to spend with the other girls, but at first I didn't feel that I was missing much. Esprit de corps was a long time in coming to our group. For one thing, we were too highly individualistic and too loosely knit to feel a deep bond, and there were very few of us who did not look upon ourselves as leaders. It may seem strange to say that I thought of myself as a leader, given the picture of the homesick, inept girl that arrived in Ireland. But after coming this far, while I would not have not described myself as a potential Joan of Arc, and I had not yet shed all those feelings of shyness and naivete of my youth, signals were rising from some place deep within that a carefully nurtured vision of a sort of undauntable real "me" that I wanted to be was trying to raise its head. I was not sure what this vision was, but after all, I reasoned, those of us who had made it thus far, unlike some who had turned back, had to have as basic ingredients determination and independence, no matter how layered over with insecurities. My convenient rationalization took the form that maturity was simply a little late in coming, blaming most of it on the ubiquitous remarks about how young I looked for my age, which at that point was not a compliment.

Another facet that worked against the group morale was that we were all thrown into this thing from greatly differing backgrounds and environments, as I have said. Much more so than the Army where an outfit was largely from one section of the country. We had girls in this group from all over the states. And while this diversity made for some interesting discoveries about the great differences based on which part of the U.S. you called home, it became apparent that the girl nurtured in the precise refinement of an Eastern girls' school found it difficult to relate immediately to the girl who had grown up in the Southwest learning to drive a tractor. And the girl who had come from a Midwestern puritanical community did not understand that the questionable oaths punctuating a southern girl's conversation were not an indication of complete moral laxity. Furthermore, as I look back now, I see that the influence of the culture which had produced us made our femininity another hurdle. Naturally so. Our culture had been quite successful in convincing us through movies and printed words that women were bound to be catty, untrustworthy, and incapable of real bonding. Movie after movie gave us a picture of male buddies bonding, but I can't think of one such movie about women, until relatively recently. This picture has changed a great deal today, but I wager that if you scratched under the skin of most of the women of my generation, and even some younger, you would still find the abiding notion, maybe unacknowledged, that women are more catty and unlike men are not to be trusted. Of course part of this scenario was that women were so dependent upon men. ("The Women" by Clare Booth Luce, a hugely successful movie in the Thirties which embodied this scenario of such catty women whose whole lives revolve around relationships with men, was recently revived to my deep groans.)

Then, too, our group was living in an intimacy that was far from comfortable to most of us. We had no room to ourselves, and we couldn't go to the bathroom alone even at those times when anyone wants privacy. And yet we had little time to get acquainted. This was particularly true of the last half of the group, for almost none of us had seen any of the rest before the trip to the Continent. And we were always surrounded by the Army; our job was to talk to soldiers not each other. For some time I feared that I would have to face up to the unpleasant truth that women did not have the capacity for group spirit, which I would hate to have to admit.

"From L to R: Jean, B.J., Doris in France"

I can almost mark the first time I felt the different spirit move among us. There was an old mine near the chateau at Jarny with a bathhouse, where the miners took their baths at the end of a dirty day in the pits. The French were allowing Americans to use it, and while a GI stood guard one night, several of us girls took over the place. The miners must have taken their baths en masse for the tubs were mammoth sunken vats, ten or fifteen feet long. Nonetheless, we took one apiece, filling them with wonderful, delicious, hot water, and wallowed.

What a heavenly experience. It had been seven weeks with no bath but one from a helmet. My body seemed something apart from me, luxuriating in a wonderful sensation even beyond what I anticipated. The other girls must have felt the same way, for as we lay there, we started to sing and as the steam rose higher our voices rose with it. The quality of our voices magically improved in this atmosphere, and by the time we got around to dressing, the guard's deep voice was chiming in from the outside. We sang all the old traditional folk songs we could think of, such as "My Bonnie Lies over the Ocean" and "There's no Place like Home." And when we stepped outside we went on to songs of the war we had recently learned—"Roll me Over in the Clover" and "Lili

Marlene"—full of well-being at having been tested and come through. This stayed with us all the way back to the chateau and at that moment I know a real togetherness was breathed into the atmosphere.

We thought nothing could be worse than the mud that came over the soles of our stadium boots, but in October the weather suddenly turned bitterly cold, and we were surprised again. As part of the process of making donut batter, one had to sift the flour using a large metal sieve, something like a gold-washing pan you see in the Westerns. I came down to the baking field one morning to find one of the girls moaning in pain, holding her hands that had gone stiff from rubbing ice cold flour against the pan. Jack remedied that by fashioning handles attached to wooden blocks for everyone, which worked as long as we needed them.

The cold brought on other problems. Some unknown crew in London had taken one of the side flaps to the cab of several of the Clubmobiles including ours. Being open to the summer air hadn't mattered, but now with the temperature going down rapidly, a flap to protect us became an important missing item. There was no such luxury as flicking on the heater so without any protection from the frigid blasts coming through the cab we arrived at our serving places with teeth chattering. Some of the crews who had not suffered the same theft took their flaps to bed with them, a not unwarranted precaution.

But eventually all of the trucks became well flapped. There were three ways of getting American goods for almost everyone in the ETO: stealing, scrounging, or bartering; all well-developed arts. Red Cross girls were not inclined to start on a career of stealing, and we were not in a good position to barter with the Army, so we refined a subtle method of resourceful scrounging or perhaps it could be called friendly bribery. In the case of the side flaps, we simply made it known to the right person at Ordnance as we handed him donuts, and not long after side flaps appeared.

Getting unnecessary goods that we all collected was a different story. We were the very willing recipients of various items from the soldiers that we cherished. "Value" took on a different meaning. An orange and a glass of cold milk, after a year or so without them, were no doubt the most valuable things I could think of but definitely not accessible. So the most esteemed available objects became things such as pistols and cameras. And we covered our jackets with medals and colorful insignias of the different divisions various soldiers gave us. We decorated the Clubmobile as well, competing with others to see who could cover the walls first.

It was at Jarny, before we were pulled back, that we were as close as we ever got to the actual front. When the Army had been racing across the continent we sometimes had to drive twenty or thirty miles to get to our destination but now we were only about fifteen miles west of the Front and were very aware of the fact. Daily we listened to the incessant pounding of guns, and sometimes a stray shell would land back where we were.

The fluidity of this thing called "The Front" amazed me. The Front was wherever there happened to be fighting. From all I had read about the first World War I had pictured a defined space, a strip of land—No Man's Land—between trenches, with opposing armies that moved back and forth fighting for that strip of land like a piece in a board game. A far cry from the present front. I'd heard about fox holes before I ever saw one but I hadn't realized what a different kind of warfare they represented. These small quickly-dug holes for a few or even a single man were very temporary, maybe overnight, shelters. And it was surprising to learn that in our war you could easily wander over into enemy territory without knowing it and not once run into barbed-wire fences.

Now we drove short distances toward the river that marks the boundary between Northeastern France and Germany: Moselle (in French) or Mosel (in German). (A very good wine comes from there, no matter which way you spell it). The river marked The Front and we passed the same signs of war day after day:

bridge after bridge that had been blown up, waving bleeding stumps of steel and concrete, warnings of dangerous, makeshift bypasses ahead. Now for some time there was no racing ahead. The Army seemed stymied for a long, long period. The city named Metz, located on the French side of the Moselle, had become the immediate goal of the Third Army since it was the last remaining Germanhold before crossing into that country, and the name became a symbol for the seemingly unobtainable.

It was about this time, we got word from Corps Headquarters to "get the hell back and quickly," so our stay with first the T.D. group and then an Armored Group came to an end. While there, we'd met a precocious little French boy who spoke English fluently (plus four other languages). Doris delighted in trying her French on him, and Jean and I practiced ours. He came to visit us each day, and his mother was happy to wash my bedroll (in exchange for a bar of soap) when I discovered bedbugs in it. When the orders came that we were to move, I had to do so with a wet bedroll after a tearful adieu from the boy.

We were in Briey back west several miles with Corps Rear when we heard that Metz was taken. Thanksgiving had come and gone, unheralded except for turkey at chow, and we were baking donuts in a garage one morning when Eva came in to tell us that the Fifth Division was already setting up a rest camp in Metz and wanted a Clubmobile there on a temporarily permanent basis, otherwise known as Detached Service, or D.S. Naturally, everyone wanted to go, and once again, those of us baking that day drew lots. By a miraculous stroke of luck, the Cedar Rapids won the draw, and we were off in a matter of minutes, bedrolls and cots slapped into the back of the truck.

"We'll be the first American women to enter Metz," Jean said savoring the thought in her manner of nonchalant but suppressed excitement.

"I bet they don't have all the snipers out yet," I gloated.

"Ooh, do you really think so?" Doris sounded as if it would be too good to be true.

I hasten to add that our attitude toward danger was one that sounds more frivolous than it actually was. Not the thrill of courting danger that a teenager finds in racing a train; it was more a feeling of wanting to prove we were capable of doing our duty, even under circumstances which we were well aware were not the same as on the front line, but still dangerous enough to warrant a show of courage. That evening, we crept into the scarred village of Metz, with its crumbling walls pierced with holes like polka dots, down the silent streets, secretly hoping we might catch sight of a sniper. His back end, of course. That night, putting up our cots in an empty room of a wing of the makeshift field hospital, we watched the nurses directing orderlies to put up their cots and bring them water and light the fires, and we whispered, "sissies" amongst ourselves.

Perhaps as retribution for that attitude about the nurses, our stay at the rest camp was disappointingly short. There was no electricity, and although our Special Services officer thought he had this under control, having captured two German generators, it seemed they spoke only German. The American GI could get them started but they never put forth enough electricity to run the donut machines. We spent the next few days chasing down rumors. Our officer wanted us to stay as badly as we did, so he did the research and come back with the results.

"There's a larger Jerry generator over at Battalion Headquarters," he'd say, and off we'd go to examine a battle-fatigued, strange-looking piece of machinery, hoping for the right number of kilocycles, watts, etc. These generators never had them though, and we finally decided that the Germans never had to warm anything up to the unreasonable temperature of 425 degrees.

Resigned, we went back to the base. The old sense of eagerness to be with the Fifth Division had to begin losing its sense of urgency. There had been so many frustrations and there would be so many more to come. Eventually as the Army became even more protective of us, there would be a few times when we'd look forward to serving a familiar battalion, only to find an officer waiting for us in a jeep to take the donuts and coffee back to the fighting company without us. And to make matters worse, not long before the Division was moved out of the XXth Corps, word came back that Company I had suffered casualties amounting to fifty per cent. And so one memorable slice of my passage to another world was laid to rest with no ceremony.

THIRTEEN

F inally, towards the end of Autumn, before snow appeared on the ground, we got orders to permanently attach ourselves to Corps Rear. From now on when they moved, we moved with them. So our next move was to barracks recently vacated by German troops in Thionville, a town in Eastern France about twenty miles south of the border of Luxembourg. We realized as we turned into the grounds of the barracks that here we would probably have a somewhat more permanent rendezvous with bare walls adorned with only the sighs of departed Germans. As it happened, the Front moved so slowly for the next few months that we spent the long winter in Thionville.

Driving in to the barren grounds, we looked with interest at the stolid, square buildings, all painted with the pink and green camouflage that sounds so deceivingly cheerful. There was nothing cheerful about these buildings. They were drab and box-like with a fearful, menacing look dictated by large black silhouettes of a sinister figure, and the inscription, "Fiend Hort Mit." (The enemy is listening, too.) We passed those signs many times a day, and it always came as a slightly bemused shock that "Fiend" and the ogre-like figure referred to us.

Three of the buildings at the end of one row were assigned to us and our GI's. They could not be called cozy but they had one very endearing feature: a toilet on each floor that worked most of the time. In addition, there was a large room in each building treated to a little pot belly stove and a basin with a spigot about two feet above it, out of which trickled water. In this room, tripping over duffle bags, we dressed and undressed and, if we had the ambition, heated water in a bucket for a sponge bath. With this new regime at Thionville we also started a new regime of our own, gleefully tearing out all the donut machines from our vehicles and putting them in a little concrete building that at one time probably had been a warehouse. Then, as soon as possible, we hired French girls to do the baking and took turns by twos overseeing them. This was much better for the machines and meant that we could serve every day instead of every other.

In spite of the comparatively comfortable accommodations, we really didn't feel lucky to be with Corps Rear. We would have much preferred to continue in the old system more on our own; and they at first didn't display much of the usual enthusiasm for having us in their back yard, either.

The jeeps that came rolling into Thionville every day with guides who took us out to their outfits wherever they were hunkered down almost invariably had occupants who said, "Hey, aren't these guys (meaning Corps Rear) lucky? How can I get a transfer to this outfit?"

But "this outfit" watched us come and go with little interest and some disdain, except for a few officers who seemed bent on adding each one of us in turn to their lists of conquests. I believe there were several reasons for the unusual lack of rapport.

The twenty or so miles between the Rear outfits with all their high brass and the line units at the front measured a far greater distance in comportment. The farther from the Front the more things became "GI"—that is, more regimented. Obviously fox holes were not subject to inspection, and nobody worried about shoes being polished on the front line, but back with Corps Rear the old Army code was strictly enforced. We Red Cross girls were civilians attached to the Army and as such, not strictly under their complete control. For instance, our barracks did not have to stand inspection. Perhaps if they had, we would not have suffered so many rats, but we preferred the rats and happily wallowed around in untidy heaps of dough-stained fatigues and open packages of food from home.

I suspect the officers felt we were a demoralizing influence due to our greater autonomy and freedom of movement. I suppose as we climbed in our drafty cabs those winter mornings and looked back with a longing shiver at the comfortable smoke curling out of the chimneys, those looks were probably matched with equally frustrated ones from the GI's stuck at a desk in the heated rooms. The GI's must have envied us our freedom, and the brass must have felt frustrated at their lack of authority over us personally. At least, we concluded that must be the reason every so often our own GI's would have to play soldier. The brass couldn't make us stand at attention for inspection so periodically they took it out on them.

Also, the fact that we had to eat in the officers' mess didn't endear us to the GI's, even if they knew we had been ordered to. During those short winter days there was little possibility of eating with the outfits we served, although we would have preferred to. With the darkness arriving so early in the day, it meant we would be driving long distances after dark without lights. Trying this once was enough. With no moon, the only way I could locate the edge of the road was by looking up at the tops of the trees on either side. Thereafter, we ate at the officers' mess.

Once we did try to protest. We were told that one of our overworked GI's would have to put in some time helping in the dining room because of the extra work we caused. Eva, who was not one to take unreasonable orders meekly, got us together and said that we would register a protest by taking our mess kits and going through the chow line with the GI's, using as rationale that this procedure would relieve them of the extra burden. As a result of this action, our GI was excused from bussing in the dining room, but the orders to eat in the officers' mess were not rescinded, so once again we were marked down as officers' girls.

Actually, this relationship, which was on a different plane from that with all other outfits, may have been a good thing to keep us all geared closer to the normal. Whenever we went elsewhere our arrival could electrify a group of men, no matter how tired and apathetic before. Sometimes it became overwhelming, almost embarrassing to see the effect your presence could inspire when they had not seen any American women for a good long time.

So perhaps a little come-uppance was in order, since there no denying that none of us ever could have been the focus of such interest before. Nor the recipient of so much fan mail. As I've said, cameras shared top honors with Lugers in barter value, and photography suddenly became the favorite hobby of practically everyone. Since taking a girl's picture was a good excuse to get her name and address, we received many copies of these pictures with accompanying letters. We considered it our duty to answer this correspondence, so much of our spare time was spent in this way. However, coming across avowals such as "you're the sweetest piece of sugar this side of heaven," we faltered as to how we should receive this news, and took quite different stances. I remember one conversation where a rather plain looking colleague tossed one of these letters aside.

"What's the matter with these guys, anyway?" she said, making a face that emphasized her point. "This is ridiculous. At home, most of them would never have looked at me. I know that. But now you'd think I'm a runner up to Marlene Dietrich."

The rest of us laughed, a bit uncomfortably, not wanting to seem impolite by agreeing with her.

But another girl who could not be thought of as particularly beautiful said, "Well, I may not get champagne all the time either, but I'll take it whenever it's offered to me and enjoy every minute of it."

And that was about as far as we were ever willing to go in analyzing this artificial phenomenon, accepting it as one more enigma of the war.

The long evenings of that winter gave Jack and me more time to be together, and after a grueling day of serving just relaxing with someone who required no effort was very welcome. As I look back now on this relationship which lasted about a year, one thing that impresses me is how little I knew about his former life. I knew he had gone to a Catholic school and that I was the first person he had ever known who believed in evolution, but we didn't spend much time discussing our previous life. The disclosure of his marriage may have played a part here, but I don't believe a very important part. It was just the ambience of the ETO that what you were before this time had lost its importance, except as a distinguishing accent of place such as naming someone "Kentucky" or "Arky." Now was now, with little thought of the past or of the future. The immediacy of war was one of its strange fruits. No planning for the future. Jack and I never thought further than our next day off when we might get to take a trip to Luxembourg, which had not been touched so much as other places by the war. It was a delight to go there just to gaze at the things for sale. One time we saw three English soldiers staring in amazement at a display in one of the stores. They turned to me asking, "Are those grips?"

"Why yes. We call them bobby pins, but I know they're 'grips' to you."

"Amazing. We haven't seen them in England for years."

A group of four of us also made a trip to Brussels on an extended weekend leave and came on a sight in one little town which brought home the quirks of war. Officials of some sort were marching a group of French women down the road with people running excitedly alongside, so we stopped to see what was going on. They told us that the women were collaborationists and were being led to prison so we'd better come and watch it. They would have their heads shaved, we were told, for having collaborated with the Germans during the occupation. There was much booing and hissing and cries damning the "Boche" aimed at the group and before we knew it we were caught up in the crowd. When we came to the prison which looked like a dusty barracks with barbed wire around it, a truck came up with some additional old women, with tears running down their faces, who had to be carried in. The booing and hissing just increased. We saw some American M.P.s taking charge of the crowd so we edged our way up to them with the help of the French people, when they saw we were Americans. The M. P. s opened the gate and let us inside to the cheers of the crowd who pointed to our cameras to indicate they wanted us to take pictures of them. The other girls turned around and as they did so all of the people automatically raised their hands in the V for victory sign. The M. P.s were almost as excitable as the people and wanted to arrange a head shaving right then for our benefit. I wrote to my family that this suggestion made me want to slink away.

"I don't want to see anyone tortured for my benefit," I wrote. "So, I was very happy to talk to the Commandant in charge, who said they would all be given a trial as there had been many innocents accused and it was difficult to pick the guilty . . . . It seems a lot of people are accused by their competitors in business or somebody who has a grudge against them. So we looked at the poor women while they read the roll call—most of them crying, some just looking sad—and left."

Today it may be hard to imagine how a mere shaving of the head could be designated as torture, when you see so many young women with coiffures so close to that description. But in those days it was a very humiliating and degrading proposition. A woman with no hair was a spectacle. I suppose one reason that we saw only women getting this treatment, besides the fact that a man's shaved head was less remarkable, was the woman's crime was more obvious; usually one of associating with a German officer. It was an easy way of getting some of the necessities of life.

Another oddity of the war was that the topic of the war itself seldom came up in any of the discussions, either in evening chats or when we went out to serve. Nobody talked about it. It just seemed there was nothing to say. It was too much with us to discuss casually. Somewhere, of course, there were people plotting and planning and very concerned with each step of the combat, but everyone we conversed with avoided any talk about the event itself. "The Stars and Stripes," the great paper published by the Army, and miraculously delivered to each outfit not at the very front, kept us abreast of what was happening so we did know what was going on. But when we went out to serve, a quick look at this paper would often tell us what was on the conversational menu for the day and without fail it would be what was going on at home. "The Stars and Stripes" had a great many different articles keeping the GIs up on the home front as well as the war, most of them very welcome. But sometimes it seemed to me that they almost went out of their way to print articles that made it tough on us girls. Stories about women with seemingly divided loyalties back home cropped up with alarming regularity. One woman helped two Italian prisoners escape from an American war prison; another ran away with a German prisoner, and there were pictures of women weeping as military officials took German prisoners away from some American internment camp.

Because we were women, it seemed we were somehow held accountable for this reprehensible state of affairs back in the states. Based on these stories, a picture developed of all the women on the home front transferring their affections en masse from the absent and forgotten Army to the enemy. I found myself constantly sticking up for the people back home, insisting these were isolated incidents, noted because they were rare. "Let's be fair" has always been my overworked slogan. Always championing a lost cause.

And by a strange chance I discovered I had collected another cause to champion without really knowing it. Somewhere along the line, the reputation of the Red Cross began to suffer some erosion. Little by little, a feeling of ill will—a chafing at the concept of THE Ideal Organization—became manifest. Not that it made much difference in our daily serving. It had no effect on the enthusiasm that always met us. But it was hard to ignore the rumors of sweaters being sold, and there was always the complaint about the charge for coffee and donuts in the clubs. Of course it did no good to try to explain that sweaters were not sold by the Red Cross but if one soldier sold a sweater he had received for free to another there was nothing to be done about it. Nor to explain that the Army made the regulation about the charge for coffee at the clubs to satisfy the English who insisted on it. I was aware of my feeling that these rumors were unfair, but gave it little thought beyond that.

But in the middle of December I found that the Red Cross had become another such cause for me without my being aware of it. It happened in a very round-about path. I had discovered some cysts at the end of my spine, and when I consulted the Corps Rear doctor, he said they were nothing serious, but should be removed so he sent me to the Station Hospital in Thionville. On December 16, in a very heavy fog, I walked into a fairly empty small tent-hospital as luxurious as tents can be. These station hospitals were one step back from the field hospitals and received those not quite so seriously injured who could be moved back from the hospitals nearest the front. Since this was a more permanent arrangement one could expect a little more professional look; this one had the air of a well kept clinic. I entered there expecting the minor surgery to keep me no longer than overnight or so. But instead, almost as soon I was examined and told to wait, the quiet little hospital became a different place. In a matter of minutes, casualties suddenly started coming in, a few at a time at first, and then one on top of another with great confusion. I overheard the staff saying over and over to each other that many of these wounded were so badly hurt they should not have been moved; a sign that the field hospitals must have been overtaxed quickly. The nurses and doctors worked feverishly and smoothly, but could not to any extent keep up with the flow. The big question on everyone's lips: "What is going on? What in God's name is going on?" We listened all day to the roar of vehicles heading north, and as a steadily increasing number of casualties came rolling in, we knew something serious was happening.

This was the beginning of "The Battle of the Bulge," the counter-offensive attempted by the Germans in the vicinity we knew so well, north of Thionville, where the famous 101st Airborne parachuted into Bastogne in the center of this area over the heads of the Germans and held it for several days. The vehicles we were hearing that day were en route to Bastogne as part of the call to concentrate all troops to push back the Germans. We know now that this breakthrough was not ultimately successful, although it did mean a loss of about six weeks in our advance across the Continent. But at that perilous moment, we couldn't foresee that, and the confusion and panic this onslaught inflicted came close to giving the German Army an edge in gaining a foothold.

This was the first time I'd come that close to seeing wounded men before they received any medical attention. I sat there in that tent, trying to make myself invisible, experiencing an overwhelming sense of agony amidst the screams of soldiers in pain. It was not just that I winced with them, but I felt so useless. If I could just have gone over and held the hand of any one of those men, torn apart with their insides hanging out, and tried to comfort him. There was nobody to do that but I had been around the hospitals long enough to know that I would be chewed out if I did anything but sit there.

At the end of the day, when things quieted down a bit, I pleaded for permission to go home: I was just taking up needed room so there was no reason I couldn't just leave and come back at a later time. But because the Army had me in its claws, I ended up two days and several hospitals later in the General Hospital in Paris—very much in everybody's way. After several days of thumb-twiddling I was told I was slated for a hospital in England. At this news, I stomped in to see the Colonel without waiting for formalities, and told him that it was senseless to waste precious plane space on me right now, that I was perfectly able-bodied, and if he would just sign my orders, I would proceed as best I could to my base and have my little operation later.

He was so surprised, I think, that he said, "We-el. It will take only a few minutes. Perhaps you'd better have it here."

So on Christmas Eve, after a heavy dose of sodium pentathol, I was back in the women's ward with the four or five nurses confined there. The drug had the usual effect, sending me into a talking jag over which I had no control. The nurses later told me, good-naturedly, that I was a big disappointment, for they had been looking forward to rummaging around in the true confessions of a Red Cross girl. But what did my subconscious contain? Any such juicy morsels? No, just a long and repetitious diatribe on the merits of the Red Cross. A Red Cross worker from Paris had appeared before me with a little Christmas gift just as I was coming to, setting off this surprising flow of emotion. I thanked her fervently and after she left declared in dramatic tones, over and over, that the Red Cross was the most wonderful organization in the whole world from Clara Barton on down, and I was proud to be a member of it. Afterwards I just felt damn silly, but recognized I had another cause to champion.

Even before this episode, I realized that I had a real group feeling, for I wished many times to be back in Thionville. I kept trying to find out what was going on but had no way to gain information. The breakthrough was occurring north and south along the road that we'd followed from Luxembourg to Brussels, but if anything was happening south of Luxembourg, I could not determine. Naturally, I pictured the worst. And I had left at the crucial hour!

After a day or so I was declared well enough to be discharged. With my papers in hand, I went back to my room, debating to myself just how I was going to get back to Thionville. I decided I would go to the Red Cross unit there in the hospital and see if they could help me. Heading for the open door, I looked up to see a familiar face. Jack!

It was a delightful surprise that took a few seconds to sink in. What a welcome sight.

"How did you get here?" I said.

"In our supply truck," Jack said, his dark eyes sparkling. "You know what I mean."

But before I could say more he swept me into his arms, with complete disregard for the rapt audience of the nurses, saying, "I thought I might not find you." He'd found out where I was through much diligence and arranged a trip to Paris to pick up supplies and me. We started out immediately, and it felt just like going home in a way; the old familiar truck with Jack headed for Thionville.

FOURTEEN

T he contented mood of home-going did not last long. The Battle of the Bulge had caused a great change in attitude because the German offensive hadn't yet been contained completely. Suspicion was the word of the day, and no longer was my uniform a symbol for relaxation and raillery. We were stopped at almost every crossroad, and the M.P.'s who stopped us now meant business. It seemed a woman in uniform was suspect, very suspect; at least, they acted more intent on questioning me than Jack, who said he had not been detained nearly so often on his way to Paris. Identification cards were of little help; they could be too easily obtained. Instead, the test for American citizenshp was to identify certain obscure American slang—not my area of expertise. I got by for a while, but as we drew closer to the Front, I started slipping.

It was getting darker, and now the snow on the ground cast everything into sharp black and white contrast. We were driving through a section where lone trees, each with a soldier standing at attention, like sentries, cast long, black shadows on the white ground. The combination of the shadows, much longer than the actual trees and the actual soldier, gave the scene an eeriness and a sense of apprehension, unlike any I had felt before. When we were stopped by the next M.P. and he made me get out of the cab for questioning, I sensed that I was about to take an important test for which I was not prepared.

"What is a fin?"

I laugh nervously. "Well, something a fish has?"

He glares back at me and waits.

"I don't know what "fin" means in slang," I say. "but before you shoot, ask me something else. Truly, I am an American. I live in Seattle, Washington. That's on the West Coast, and you can see I don't have an accent, because we don't on the West Coast, and . . ."

I stop, realizing I am being foolish.

After a few more dirty looks, he resumes questioning, and because I do know what a "buck," a "grand," and "two bits" are, he is satisfied and lets me go.

Jack hooted and hollered at my stupidity and spent the rest of the trip coaching me on baseball terms, underworld lingo, and other bits of Americana. We made it back without any more slips.

When we got back to Thionville suddenly everyone seemed like real friends, the palpable camaraderie especially welcome after my adventures in the hospital and the M.P.s' cold appraisal of me as a possible enemy. I understood then why so many GI replacements, coming back for a second time, went AWOL when the only alternative was to join a different outfit. The familiarity and rapport of friends and fellow soldiers was important for survival.

After the breakthrough, as the front moved with increasing rapidity towards the Rhineland, our daily journeys got longer and longer. Sometimes we'd drive fifty miles each way before returning to Thionville; we were attached to Corps Rear so firmly we couldn't move until they did. To avoid the long drives we began staying overnight at our destinations, packing a larger supply of donuts in the morning or sending a jeep back to Thionville for more. Taking our cots and bedrolls with us now, we spent the nights in barren buildings that'd been evacuated by the Germans or in old barns or Nissen Huts or sometimes at the Field Hospitals, where we slept in the nurses' quarters. Only the most critical patients were cared for at these facilities, so the staffs were small and the nurses were truly glad to see other American women, cordially inviting us to watch operations when our day was over.

Several times, with a white rag over my mouth, I watched as two exhausted doctors performed the most serious of operations in an old tent, or an old room in a Nissen Hut, making use of a bare bulb for light, usually amidst great confusion and noise on the other side of the door or flap. Those doctors earned all the kudos they ever got.

The first time I observed such an operation, I watched a doctor work on a very young blonde soldier whose torso had been blown open, like so many I had seen that first day of the Bulge. This was far from a clean, tidy incision and stitch job. The soldier's innards spilled out of the wound and had to be stitched together first and then stuffed back in the wound. As I watched, the first thing the doctor did was to snip off a floating rib and throw into the garbage as something useless to be thrown away; a little shock of surprise etched that gesture into my brain. And by the time the operation was over the young man had become a person to me; I had become invested in his outcome. The following morning I asked after him and was told that he'd died of pneumonia.

"That's what happens to most of them," the nurse said. "They die of pneumonia, not the wound."

I nodded glumly, and turned away.

No further observation of an operation would grip me like that one, of course. It became possible to watch with an interest and objectivity almost matching that of the doctors and nurses. And eventually towards the end of that winter I began to wonder about this. Had we all become hard-hearted? Was this the inescapable result of being at war?

On a cold, cold day when the barracks at Thionville seemed a good deal less than cozy, I was staring out the window and happened to look down at the ledge below. It was covered with the dead rats that had made our uninspected large room their home; rats we had killed and nonchalantly tossed out the window as just another part of the routine. We have come a long way, I thought. But towards what? No doubt it was an advance of some kind that we could kill rats with aplomb instead of just standing and screeching. But was this just part of a larger transition, a drift into accepting anything that comes along, without registering any feeling? I couldn't think of this as an admirable advance.

This mood stayed with me when we went out to serve the next day. As it happened, we got behind a graves registration vehicle carrying its load of American corpses. They were uncovered because they were frozen stiff, and they bounced up and down like wooden logs. We had to follow them for a long distance and somehow this cargo I was seeing, as if for the first time, became the symbol of what I was feeling: that these corpses might as well have been frozen fish; that we had all gotten so inured we paid little attention and cared less.

"It's all so organized," I said aloud.

My co-workers looked at me quizzically, probably thinking that organized murder was not an original description of war.

"What's so organized? The war?" Doris said.

"Well, yes, I mean," I gestured towards the truck ahead. "There are those bodies, as if they were pounds of fish being delivered to—to a customer. All so efficient, so unfeeling. And we just accept it as normal."

"What else can we do?" Jean asked. "You can't let it get to you, or you'll just end up no good. Right?"

I knew she was right, and I had no other words to express what I had in mind. I was thinking of the many impassive faces I had seen under any and all circumstances. I had visions of a huge machine, whose purpose was to spew out people to be rolled down an assembly line, some to graves registration and some to a hospital where another assembly line waited to try to put back together the pieces that had been systematically torn asunder— not by accident, but by design. All so well organized, so mechanical.

As we followed the corpses down the road, I also thought about an item in the "Stars & Stripes" by a GI bemoaning the fact that henceforward, after experiencing the carnage of combat, he would find it impossible to show any sympathy to his wife over a small accident like cutting her hand. Maybe so, I thought. Were we becoming hardhearted? Will it be that compassion will have left us? Was that the conversion we would carry home?

I felt confusion over this for some time, although now I'm certain that the GI's predictions were off. I recognize now that what I and the GI had mistaken for a permanent hardness of heart was nature's way of shutting down temporarily in order to keep that part of the brain intact—but only temporarily. In other words, this "hardening" process was a transient necessity to keep the psyche from disintegrating. One cannot keep reacting emotionally constantly, when confronted with overwhelming stimuli. In this case, an emotion will become unglued to thought, going on to combust by itself, with no present stimulus. In World War I they spoke of "shell-shock." In our war we dealt with "battle fatigue." Now they talk about "traumatic stress disorder." Each war, I guess, will have its term for the psychological maiming dealt to a great many of the combatants; a cost not tallied for its true expense. I recall that during my first reunion with Company I the kitchen crew told me about one casualty, a man who had for no sensible reason rushed up a hill purposely exposing himself by standing straight up and yelling like a banshee.

Another part of the problem with this confusion about the deadening of feelings, I believe, is the common perception that it is weak or unmanly to show emotion, particularly to cry. My very first encounter with a grown man crying uncontrollably came not long after we arrived in France before we caught up with the Corps. We had come in contact with some members of the French Resistance and one day, while we were waiting for supplies, we were sitting in a cafe talking to some of them. This one Frenchman, who had been joking with us, suddenly turned serious and started talking about the many French children who had suffered malnutrition and died during the occupation. Abruptly, he simply laid his head, in its red, white and blue sailor cap, down on the table and started sobbing loudly. I had never before seen a man let himself go like that in public and it thoroughly embarrassed me. At the time I just put it down to another difference in culture.

It may have been true that there was a difference in culture, but I see now that I had been conditioned to accept the American ethic that real men (and real men are the superior human beings) don't cry. In the states it was thought "unmanly" for a man to cry. Those of my generation can all remember how Edmund Muskie, a presidential candidate, was caught on television with tears in is eyes because of an attack on his wife; and how his run for presidency was then derailed. Since then it gradually became more acceptable for a man to show some emotion; it was asserted with approval that he was getting in touch with his feminine side. However, it has become manifest that there is a backlash against this new outlook. Especially since 9/11, with the show of strength and heroism on the part of the firefighters and policemen, a grateful public has often responded by a call for returning to the recognition of our strong men as heroes that exemplify the best there is. "Macho" is back in. Enough of this gushing with emotion. Let's not try to make them less "manly" by turning to their weaker feminine side. And there's the rub. The weaker-feminine side.

Words direct our perception much more than is commonly understood. To be "manly" is to be strong and courageous; to be "unmanly" is to be effeminate or cowardly (according to the dictionary.) And effeminate means "qualities more often associated with women than men; characterized by weakness." This sensitive, caring, gushy side: this is just the weaker side. By the same token "womanly" means "having the becoming qualities of a woman." Whatever qualities these are, they are not the qualities of an ideal human being. (I'm tempted to ask: becoming to whom?)

No doubt women are weaker than men physically. And they cry more easily. Granted. Males, when they are very young are taught to be brave and not cry when they are hurt. To stifle your sobs when in pain is "being a brave little man." So crying becomes a sign of cowardice. But most women are not held to the same standard, (though I think they should be.) So crying, the sign of weakness and cowardice becomes effeminate. But actually in adults, crying is seldom the response to personal physical paiin. More often than not, it is a sympathetic response to someone else's pain. And here we can run into trouble. Is sympathy and sensitivity to other peoples' feelings expressed by tears an indication of weakness? Well, it can be.

Emotion that is not connected to thought does becomes a "gushy" weakness. For example, my very young daughter once came home, weeping copiously, with a dead rabbit in her arms that she had picked up off the street. I couldn't help smiling to myself at the irony, for the dead rabbit's blood had spilled over her favorite white rabbit jacket she was wearing. Of course she was much too young to see any link. But if she had gone on crying at every animal she saw run over in the street, she would indeed be exhibiting the weakness of never growing up. And the person who sheds buckets of tears over a "tear jerker" movie is responding in the same way; immaturely. A movie calculated to do just that—jerk your tears—without real substance is cheating. The overwhelming emotion is inappropriate to the stimulus. Someone tagged this sort of stimulus "emotional porn." But this emotional reponse is as inappropriate for females as it is for males. Just as we had to shut down our emotions, during the war, to protect our psyche lest they become unglued to thought, so it is important to maintain the connection to thought in the everyday world in order to act as a mature human being.

If only we had a word that would mean "ideally human, whether male or female." Then maybe we would see that women should aspire to be courageous and have strength of character (strength is not merely physical) and men should not eschew compassion and sensitivity to the feelings of others. Only a tyrant, who is less than human, lacks the ability to shed tears for others' plight under the right circumstances. The ideal, aspired to as a complete human being, would embody traits considered to be "manly" and equally traits considered to belong to women. Which the label "womanly" does not do.

Ernie Pyle, the great WW II journalist knew that war was not glamorous. As he pointed out again and again, monotony was the true bete noir of the infantryman. The many movies about the War (or any war for that matter) could never bring this out. Watch any of them and you would think that the fighting was almost constant. After all, movies demand action, and pictures of boredom do not sell. But the reality was that most of the time monotony was the cruel companion. The same old misery day after day, with no variety becomes very hard to take. By the middle of the winter, it seemed apathy had taken over everywhere, which even our presence was not always able to dispel.

And for us, too, the next few weeks were spent, in much less difficult circumstances, treading time, doing the same thing day after day. The same long, cold rides, the same troops waiting for us with different individuals, but pretty much distinctive over-all personalities—some outfits taking on an almost feverish attitude of "seizing the day," and others falling into complete apathy where nothing seemed to matter much. These attitudes seemed to be contagious. And always we kept up the smiling as best we could, trying in some way to buoy up spirits that had so little reason to be uplifted.

One real frustration that winter was the occasional loss of our record player. The grease lubricating the winding spring would solidify, and we'd have no music. On these occasions Doris and I had a repertoire of two pieces that we'd harmonize over the microphone. We did not expect to be received like the Andrews sisters, but sometimes we were successful in that we gave courage to someone to display a small talent. If we were lucky, it grew into an impromptu jam session. Then, the only discouraging feature was that we'd have to quit and pack up just as we were all getting in the groove.

On a personal level the D.S. arrangement had another slightly unexpected side effect. It developed that Jack was not happy about my being away from him so much of the time. He complained that he worried about me, and that I stayed out later than he deemed necessary. Furthermore, he said it didn't seem to bother me; if it did, I would make more effort to hurry home to him. Strange, I thought, here our roles are sort of reversed. He was at home waiting for me to return from work. So he acts like the married woman whose husband leaves her alone too much of the time. And like the proverbial husband I could not deny that I began to feel a leash-like constraint. An odd state of affairs that worked itself into the background where it shortly became unnoticeable, because spring and the promise of change was concentrating our attention.

We were so anxious for some diversity we got out the paint can long before it was painting weather and tried to spruce up our Clubmobiles. One of our favorite phrases was "beat up," and our Clubmobiles had become the epitome of "beat up" which some of us tried to amend. Dainty trims of bright red and orange were popular, because that was the paint that was available. It was a contest to see who could be the most artistic with the limited resources. To be sure, there were some who felt the "beatuppness" should be worn like a badge, even cultivated, but the Cedar Rapids crew was not among them. We painted wherever we could, and the most important feature was the map of the U.S. with the spots marked so that we could point when asked "Where are you from?" The freehand map was not exactly to scale and Florida looked decidedly oversized, but it did avoid the monotony of the question until the map finally became illegible.

Spring also brought a more vigorous crop of rumors. At times, because we'd worked through the same routine for so long, just as in Ireland, it seemed hard to believe that life would not go on the same old way forever; yet there were unmistakable signs of change. For one thing, the definite esprit de corps which had crept into our ranks. We started to have birthday parties and we lingered a bit longer after meetings, ignoring the whistling and stomping feet outside the barracks. It had become a real pleasure to have an exclusively feminine world for a few minutes. They were singing, "They're Either too Young or too Old" back home, but we seldom saw anyone under eighteen or over thirty five and all of them male. Most of our serving was being done in Germany now, and the civilians had vanished or were boarded up in one building, bringing home the fact that it's pleasant to have equal amounts of old and young, male and female. Perhaps that's why the GI's were famous for being kind to children and old people. They missed them.

Everyone was chafing at the bit for change, but when the order finally came that we were to move into Germany, we acted as people usually do who are leaving places and experiences, either sweet or bitter, behind. After we'd snapped all the pictures we felt necessary, acquired our laundry from all the different French homes, and taken our last look around Thionville, we were prepared to start out in convoy once again. We unanimously decided to invite the French girls along to bake our donuts, and they accepted eagerly.

We drove out the gates of the Thionville compound with ambivalent emotions, reinforced by the large signs posted at the border of France. "You are Now Entering Germany. Be on Your Guard. Don't Fraternize." We had passed it many times before on day trips to serve the different units, but this time it was for good. We snapped photos of it, so we'd never forget.

Then began again the slow lumbering across the map, the stopping for one flat tire, the looking for fields large enough to park our trucks, the K rations, and the waiting while someone dashed off in the jeep to see if we were on the right road. Only now there were no bottles of champagne, no cheering, no smiling children by the side of the road, and our irritability at the end of a day was only from fatigue, not excitement.

Our own troops passing by became less responsive. The mechanized divisions still had energy to cheer and wave with some enthusiasm, but without looking at the markings on the trucks, we could spot an infantry outfit that was being moved by the weariness about them. A dreary indifference seemed to surround them. Their mouths sagged. Their eyelids drooped. Their heads lolled. Only their beards flourished. It was hard to look at them without agonizing for them and without feeling some inadequacy.

Those weeks we spent tugging ourselves across Germany, trying to keep up with the hurtling Army and still keep our donuts rolling, were marked by more confusion. Not the same kind of confused excitement accompanying our first pull across the continent; it was more a matter of not being able to sort out our reactions. This trip we did not have to sleep on the ground since the conquering Army could take over any place they wanted, and turn it over to us. Often we moved into a house where the Army had not yet ousted the inhabitants, and it was painful to watch as they were forced to leave their home. We'd look the other way as long as possible, but inevitably a woman, more often than not with a pink scalp showing through her thinning white hair, would show surprise at seeing it was her own sex ousting her. Then with her manner showing a fllck of hope that we might be more receptive than the soldiers, she would grab one of us by the arm and beg us to water her plants, or feed her cat or take care of something precious. Whether in German or English, the message got through, and then ambivalence and confusion arose, and our sense of purpose disintegrated. I suspect I was not the only one whose consciousness was crowded by many a ghost of World War I writers. They'd convinced us that the enemy was not the German people, as such, and that all men are brothers if you take them one at a time. But, crowding in on these ghosts were the more recent ones of the torn bodies and all the dead soldiers so quickly forgotten and hauled around like debris.

And then there was the confusing rule of non-fraternization. To be strictly enforced, it said, on practically every telephone pole. Further, many a poster pointed out the danger of breaking this rule because the seductive fraulein could cry "Rape"—a court-martial offense. However, we knew the rule was hardly being observed.

"Oh, they make me so mad sometimes," one girl says of the soldiers after a day of serving. "Half of those guys walking away with a helmetful of donuts. I say to them, 'Hey, where're you going with those donuts?' And they just smile and say, 'We've gotta couple of buddies.' So I say, 'Yeah. I know all about your buddies. You listen to me. The Red Cross didn't send us over here to feed German frauleins'. But what can you do? They just smile at you and look as if they thought you were jealous or some damn thing."

"Well, if the Army hadn't made such a ridiculous rule," Dee offers, "there wouldn't be all this trouble. How did they ever think they could stop it? That just makes it more tempting. Honestly, simply honestly."

And by the time we arrived in Munich, the Army, too, must have thought it a losing proposition, for there nailed on the same telephone pole were two signs, one under the other: the top one: "Non-Fraternization will be Strictly Enforced" and right under it, the one familiar from France where condoms were handed out freely "Pro Station—One Block" (Pro = prophylactic) with an arrow pointing the way. We laughed a laugh of cynicism.

Then of course there was a much worse confusion, soon after we entered Germany. At first, we ran into the Americans being liberated from the P.O.W. camps. In general, they looked merely thin, compared to what we saw soon after. Now, after so much notoriety, It may be hard to imagine that we knew nothing about the concentration camps and how incredible the news of such places seemed. At first we didn't know what to make of the rumors. One after another, soldiers told us with stricken eyes, "Don't go near that place. You don't want to see it." That place was the now-famous Dachau. I wrote to my parents at this time when the news of these ghastly places was beginning to filter through to them. I said that the men who had been there were so obviously devastated by what they'd seen that we took their advice to stay away.

I continued, "I probably would not have followed this advice a year ago. I would just have gone anyway. But now I have seen enough, and have no desire to go looking for more horrors."

Still, since we were stationed not far from there, we began to see some of the actual survivors of this infamous camp. So hard to believe; to realize that this could happen to people. We didn't discuss it: it was beyond our ability to put into words. We just looked in amazement. We were asked a couple of times to serve some of them who were still ambulatory as they waited for transportation, and one time we came across a tent filled with such litter cases in one of the Field Hospitals. I'm not sure whose idea it was to feed these victims donuts, as if they'd be able to digest them, but in the confusion at the time we complied with the requests, only to watch with real apprehension as these poor live skeletons wolfed them down. We tried to warn them, thinking of the result that must ensue, but almost all of them who could, opted for taking the consequences. It was easy to understand their desire for anything to eat.

Since, whenever I've seen a film about the concentration camps, I've been struck by the great divide between the representation and the reality. Even though it's possible to do a pretty accurate job of making the actors look thin and gaunt, the true appearance could never be reached. You might think a neck doesn't have much meat on it, but without any meat at all, it is a haunting apparition, a thin, thin, scrawny stick that looks so fragile it might break from the effort to hold up a head. The image has never left me.

FIFTEEN

The "Battle of the Bulge," proved to be the last real threat to the continuous advance of our army, and as we came into the longer days of spring, there was little doubt that the end had to come soon. We knew it could not be long, if for no other reason than the Germans had to be running out of soldiers. Every day we passed truck-load after truck-load of German prisoners, who added one more straw to our confusion by merrily waving to us. I think they just could not contain their joy and relief at being alive with the end in sight. We were getting very impatient for the war to end, and when it did come, the ending was very anticlimactic. There was much confusion about which day was to be celebrated. Should it be the day, May 7, when we heard the surrender was to be signed? Or should we wait for the next day when it was to be effective? Or what?

My sister wrote to me about the glad tidings. "Of course," she said."If it was exciting to us, it must have been more so to you. I can see you now throwing your arms around everybody and jumping up and down. What an exciting day that must have been."

And I suppose it was rather cruel of me to write and tell her the whole truth, that I'd had my arms around a donut machine when a GI walked in and said, "Well. I guess it's confirmed. It's all over."

"You sure?" I asked.

"Yeah. I heard it on the radio. Not that it makes much

difference to me. We'll be here for years yet or sent over to Japan. Besides it still has to be ratified or something."

"At least the fighting's over. It may not mean much to you but it will make a big difference to the guys out on the front, you know." I said. "Want a donut?"

The next day someone else came by complaining because he'd been saving a bottle of Scotch for the big event for months, but now he'd gone ahead and drunk it yesterday thinking it was official, and so he had nothing for today.

VE Day, however, did mark an abrupt change in the make up of our group. There were several girls who had already spent their two years on this side of the ocean, and had been bucking to get home for some time. VE Day was the go-ahead signal for them, and a few days later we waved goodbye.

Jean was being very quiet in the hospital with diphtheria, and after we went to see her, Doris mentioned half-seriously that she envied her getting to spend a week or so in bed. That made me think of the Red Cross home in England where you could get breakfast in bed. And hey, I had a leave coming. The next day I was on my way. I went out to the Air Field, found a pilot who was going to Paris, and went along. It was that easy when there was just one of you. All you needed was traveling orders, and you could always be squeezed into the cockpit. I was very glad it was the cockpit on this particular trip, since the cargo was a group of French prisoners being returned to their homeland. They'd been liberated from one of the concentration camps and while one could only look at them with compassion, one could only gag at the overpowering odor clinging to them.

The trip from Paris to London was almost as simple, and once there I found it delightful to be back in England. Almost like coming home. It was a real pleasure to walk down the street amidst a civilian population that didn't look the other way when you approached.

Surprisingly though, when I talked to my Red Cross cohorts, I felt quite out of joint. The club was one maintained by the Red Cross for its personnel on leave or en route from one assignment to another. Hardly had I stepped foot in the door, when I found myself being ushered in to the dining room where lunch was being served, and with a grand flourish, introduced with the remark, "She's been on the Continent."

"You have? Where? Tell us all about it," the girls clamored.

Well, there was nothing wrong with that. But I didn't get very far without running into stumbling blocks.

"Must've been exciting to be right there on VE Day," they said. "Gee, I wish I'd been there."

"Well, as a matter of fact, it was probably much more exciting right here in London," I said. "You see . . . . after all, don't forget the Germans have nothing to celebrate and there we are in the midst of them. It's a little difficult to have too much celebration and then . . . We knew it was coming for so long it was sort of an anti-climax."

"Well, yes," they said. "But we knew it was coming, too. And, oh dear, to be right there and know it's over. It had to be exciting."

There was a green salad in front of me, which I was eyeing with lustful glances.

"You don't know how good this looks to me," I said.

"This?" they cried. "Water cress? Surely, you had better food in France than we get here! I don't care if it's shoe leather, the French will make it taste better than the English food."

"But we didn't get much French food. We ate with the Army, you know."

"Well, even the Army has better food than the English."

I thought back to the Army mess hall, "Willow Run" in London, and how much the English appreciated an invitation there with its appetizing food.

"Well, that was true here, of course," I said. "But the rations over there aren't quite so good."

"And then tell us," they continued. "What's this we hear about looting. That's exaggerated, isn't it?"

"Perhaps a little, but you know, when you see a roomful of

loot that has been taken from the French with the franc marks still on it . . . well, there's some excuse."

"Still, surely our GI's wouldn't walk into a German home and take things?"

I gave my attention to my salad.

By the end of the luncheon they didn't want to hear any more of my answers to their questions. And for the rest of my stay there I feigned complete exhaustion or battle fatigue and gained the solitude, which was what I really wanted.

Getting back to Germany wasn't as easy as the trip out, but after several flights and many hundreds of miles out of my way, I made it back to the Seventh Army Headquarters, which I thought was as good as any place to find out where my group was. I reasoned rightly that it had probably moved while I was gone. With the help of a Transportation Officer, I made contact with the Third Army and the XXth Corps and found out that my Group H was stationed in Reid, not far from Munich. I stood talking to the officer just after we had made this contact, when two lively young girls in the Red Cross uniform came shuffling in the door announcing that they were looking for Group H. They turned out to be replacements for some of the girls who had left, and in short order, the officer gave us a couple of drivers with a weapons carrier and sent us on our way. Barbara and Portia were long time friends and were fond of kidding each other so we had a seemingly short drive back to Reid.

Upon our arrival we found that Eva and Angela had decided it was time for a shake-up; that we probably needed a change from listening to the same old line of chatter and there were several new girls who needed to be with a veteran to show them the ropes. I was happy to find that Barbara and Portia were to be on my crew. They were so fresh and animated that though they made me feel like a hardened veteran, they also brightened my outlook.

Now that the Army was an Army of Occupation, a collective energy rose from the ashes of waiting for the war to end. We easily slipped back into the early enthusiasm of kidding and badinage, both with the troops and each other. The three of us had no trouble in finding something to laugh about. And now that it was all over, the group as a whole drew even closer together. We had more frequent gabfests over the champagne that we still managed to acquire, and there was that spirit in the air. "Well, old gal, after all, there may have been times when I didn't know about you, but we did come through this thing together. Something to be proud of, don't you know?"

This feeling even extended to Corps Rear. Now the soldiers would come to have their pictures taken with us just like everybody else. Furthermore, when we moved again, those in command gave us some of the better spots. They'd been looking for a more inviting site than Reid for their permanent headquarters and they picked a glorious one, Starnberg on the Wurmsee. They had given us, overlooking a little jewel of a lake, three beautiful homes, a small one for the supervisors, one for our five GI's and a mansion for the general group.

This mansion was more fabulous then the chateau in Jarny, for it looked just as good on the inside as it did on the outside. It still had its plush furniture and two, not one but two, beautiful lovely bathrooms. The kitchen, as usual, was in a damp, barren cellar with several small rooms leading off it, and it seemed the logical place to quarter our French girls to make our donuts. This was rather unfortunate, however, because it had doors leading to the outside so we had no way of keeping track of who came and went. We finally had to put our collective feet down. We explained to the French girls that we were not interested in their off-duty behavior, but for the sake of our reputation it was necessary to make certain that no man was seen wandering in or out of our house at odd hours, odd hours being those between one and seven a.m. This arrangement they found very unsatisfactory.

As Marie bitterly put it one day, "Quelle vie! Manger, travailler, coucher. C'est tout. Quelle vie!"

They were very unhappy and getting weary of donuts. We couldn't blame them, so when one of the Simones, (the one whose face would have been described as beautiful except for a permanently petulant look) resigned from her job to go off and live in style with her officer, we were not surprised. Then we discovered that the temptation of our supplies had been too much for them, (lard, soap and coffee made wonderful bartering material) so we decided it was best to send them back home.

When word got out that we would be hiring German girls to replace them, we were besieged with applications which the Burgomeister had cleared and presented to us as suitable. We also hired two Rumanian displaced persons, a young boy and his sister, who had come out of a concentration camp and walked until they found each other—the only two left of their whole family. They had been wandering around the countryside for months with no place to go, so it was gratifying to be able to help them out. Sandy, the brother showed his appreciation by making little boxes for Eva and me with our names, dates, and Starnberg carved on them. It was disheartening to me how quickly these people became known as "D.P.'s" with the accompanying pejorative sense.

All of these new employees were very grateful for the job and to have the chance to sample their product. It seemed that lard must have been one staple there was a dearth of in Germany, for these girls gobbled it down like candy. One day I saw Tuck, one of our GI's, sharing a lard sandwich with one of these bakers, a flaxen-haired girl with a pleasant round face. I figured he was really smitten.

With this house to come back to and the blossoming of a true camaraderie, all of us looked forward to the return from D. S. now. But there was another very important reason, and that was that about two weeks of D. S. was all we could take. For this period was the most fatiguing of our whole overseas experience. We thought that it would be nice to settle down again while we were dragging our weary selves across Germany, but we didn't realize what it would entail. Now, a division was spread over a good portion of the map, well settled down and very ready for recreation. The Special Services Officer had our program all plotted out for us and enthusiastically outlined it on the map.

"Now, we'll serve this Battalion on Monday, stay at Company B, and then move on to this Battalion fifty miles away and you can stay there with Company K, and we'll pick up Headquarters the next day. It's just twenty miles away and the Colonel has a wonderful little house for you there."

In the face of this enthusiasm, we could not let him know that our knees got weak just thinking of it. Because naturally, Company B would go all out for us Monday night, and we'd stay up until one or two dancing and listening to their talent. A long drive ahead of us the next day would mean starting out at 7:30, followed by a long day of serving, and naturally Company K would go all out for us Tuesday night, and we'd get to bed at one or two. And the Colonel's private little house meant it would be full of male laughter until midnight at least. And how could we plead fatigue when it was such a special occasion for them? At the end of two weeks, we'd flop down beside the lake and declare we wouldn't move for two days.

By the second day of rest, however, we usually found that we could move after all, and we would start out on our new-found activity: scrounging up clothes. After a year of muddy trousers and long Johns, everyone was willing to go to almost any length to get a frill or two. We all had some contraband civilian clothes lying in a box in London, but appeals to have them sent to us now that the war was over fell on deaf ears, so we had to look elsewhere. We had in our possession several bolts of cloth donated to us by the Army as unwanted loot from a warehouse, and with these in hand, we'd start out in search of a tailor or seamstress.

We followed in the GI's wake but not with the same success. For some reason the Frau even while working on an American uniform would shake her head "Nicht Verstehe." Our German was not exactly fluent, but in the end, after many tries we did have some success. Barbara, Portia, and I were particularly fond of dirndls we achieved out of some tablecloths and draperies. I don't believe they were the best illustrations of the original Bavarian dirndl, but we thought them very chic. Within the confines of our own grounds we got great pleasure, donning these clothes and sticking a flower in our hair. We hesitated before wearing them farther afield, for the few times we did, even GI's who knew us mistook us for German girls, and it embarrassed them mightily when they slammed on the brakes, saying, "Vee Gates?" to discover us. We felt it kinder not to force the issue.

In addition, there was another motive in wanting to be easily recognizable. I felt it would be nice to have a flashing sign saying, "I understand English," because the Army seemed to believe that no Germans could. At least, they were all using the same language that they used when alone but heretofore would clean up for us. Now, if they couldn't tell we were Americans it could become rather embarrassing. It would not have mattered so much for us alone, because our own conversation was studded with words that would have been deplored by our mothers and we were far beyond the shock stage I had experienced in Ireland, but in the company of a GI it could become an Emily Post nightmare. For instance, one evening which threatened rain, I was walking down the street with my GI date. We stopped across the street from his quarters and he pointed out his room. Almost immediately several of his buddies appeared at the windows shouting remarks that made it obvious that they thought I was German, unable to understand what they were saying. They were puzzled by his being seen so openly with me, (because of the non-fraternization rule) and they wondered what enticement this babe had proffered that would make him take such a chance. I quickly realized that my raincoat had no outstanding identification, so I spoke up with vehemence.

"Hey, you guys," I shouted, "I am American. But what if I weren't? Some Germans do understand English, you know."

There was no answer, except shocked silence and closing of windows. I looked at my companion with sympathy. He was the kind who embarrassed easily, and could manage nothing but confused silence. We wandered on for some time before conversation became normal again.

SIXTEEN

On August 6 of that summer of 1945, the news in the "Stars and Stripes," was cataclysmic. I don't know which was the greater surprise—that there was such a thing as the Atom Bomb, or that our country would use it on a city of civilians like Hiroshima. It was strange to be in occupied Germany and get this news. We looked at each other with blank faces, to be filled in later. There was elation that it marked the end of the War, but there was also bewilderment about the means employed. The mixed feelings were only magnified three days later with the hit on Nagasaki. We knew our world had changed again and permanently. It weighed heavily on my mind. It seemed to me the change brought about by the War was now out-stripped by the magnitude of this new dimension. I wished that I had my family to discuss it with. Whereas we had been so morally certain that this was a "just" war, this event coming as the result of it threw me off base and talking it over with others didn't help much, because no one seemed to have a decided conviction.

On my first day off after this news, I went swimming with Jack in the Wurmsee, which was one of the perks of our site at Starnberg. Because of the D. S. set-up, we were perforce seeing less and less of each other, and with the end of the war it seemed we had come to a shared equanimity about facing the future of a different path without each other. Still, I felt close enough to turn to him in giving vent to my concerns; similar at that time to conversations going on all over the world, I'm sure.

"From L to R: Barbara, Portia, B.J. In Germany"

"Why couldn't they have given some warning first?" I fumed. "Why couldn't we have dropped one of these horrendous things nearby on an uninhabited island or something to show them what would happen if they didn't surrender? It just doesn't seem right to drop it on women and children and old men when they're not fighting a war. They're civilians," I protested from the depth of my shaken sense of "fair is fair."

"Well, what do you think the people in London were?" Jack said, in his matter of fact way. "Did that stop the Nazis? And you've seen Munich. Do you think there was nobody there when we bombed it to pieces? Lives are lives. Anything is fair in love and war. Furthermore . . . ." Jack shrugged his shoulders. "Maybe the first bomb didn't do it. I guess It took two."

"But this seems so much worse than plain old bombs," I said. "And little children . . . I don't know. I suppose it's true that there is no real difference between killing civilians and soldiers. But they didn't have a chance. They were innocent bystanders." It crossed my mind that Jack, like all of Corps Rear, had a different experience of the war than those on the front lines. They were even more sheltered than we had been from its ferocity.

"What is an innocent bystander?" he said. "Anyone without a

gun? How about the people in London or some of those other places? They were innocent bystanders, too, then. Anyway it's done and there's nothing you can do about it. Just be glad the fighting is going to stop."

Little did we dream that fifty years later, war would take the turn of civilian against civilian. And that the young people willing to commit suicide to kill other civilians believe they are doing it to the dictates of their God.

We could not know, at the time, whether this new weapon was so bad that it would prevent another war, as some were saying, or could be banned as others believed. Yet, I think that in the deep recesses of my concern lay the new and fearful realization that this war, which we believed so just and righteous, had resulted in something that could never be taken back, and that mankind was not ready for.

We were sitting on the dock dabbling our feet in the water on the little dock attached to the house which had been assigned to our GI's. I did not feel reassured by this conversation but Jack gave me a bucking-up pat on the shoulder and dove into the clear, blue water. I followed, and after a few laps, feeling much refreshed, we climbed out and stretched out comfortably side by side in the wonderful sunshine.

There has always been something about lying in the sun after a dip in the water that is great solace to my spirit. (Later, much later, I found it one of the great disappointments in life to be denied this essential therapy to the inner self because of the detriment to the outer self.) That day in particular I recall the recognition that the sun beating down on me had shone on this world and all its calamities and cruelties undisturbed since the beginning of time, and would go on doing so no matter what happened. Even if we, as a species, were determined to blow ourselves out of existence. One often hears of people experiencing this sort of sensation, usually described as feeling "at one with the universe." Ordinarily it is described as a feeling of smallness, like a grain of sand of no significance. To me it seemed more like a sense of empowerment: that the small grain of sand I call "myself" is no more but no less than any other, and therefore just as significant in the scheme of things, recognizing that all the frustrations and tribulations encountered are mere blips in the huge mystery. The only course of action is to keep curious and interested. Right then, that thought felt as comforting as the sun. I rolled over and dozed off.

An even greater change came about in my routine because, to my great surprise, I was offered the job of co-supervisor for the group. Even though I knew I'd miss the actual serving of the men, I felt I could not pass up this honor, sure evidence that I'd not failed in this overseas adventure. I threw myself as wholeheartedly as I could into being a supervisor. As other gals went home, several more replacements came, and I met them at the train in Munich, herded them back home, answered their questions, coached them on their jobs and listened to their bubbling enthusiasm with the amused indulgence becoming an old veteran. Two years from freshman to senior.

A little later I had a real reason to regret having left my Clubmobile. Portia and Barbara, were operating as a duo without me, and if I'd stayed on the "Cedar Rapids" maybe, with three of us, that day would have turned out differently. As it was, on a very rainy day they went out to serve and Portia's hat blew out of the cab. She jumped out of the truck and ran back to get it. It was back farther than she expected, so she called to Barbara to come and get her. It was not yet autumn but already the road was thickly covered with wet leaves, and somehow Portia slipped on them and was under the truck before Barbara could stop it. The huge dual tires ran over her pelvis. For five days, we lived on the edge of hope, trying to make ourselves believe she would make it. Portia was lovable and witty and could not, just could not, be gone in this way—so needlessly and after the war was over. But her body had been too badly crushed.

I came in to the big house the day after we learned that Portia had died, just as Barbara was waking up from a nap on the sofa.

Unaware that I was there, she stretched out her arms with a little yawn and opened her eyes, at first quite naturally. Then the sudden awareness of where she was came over her, and her expression changed dramatically with eyes darkened as if she were looking into an abyss of horror. And of course she was—the realization of the nightmare awaiting her in the real world; the awareness that she was responsible for an unnecessary death made it seem worse than the death that had been all around us.

We arranged a funeral for Portia, but since none of the amenities for funerals were available in the ETO, those arrangements were very difficult. Embalming was out of the question and it was warm weather. This was one time I felt that I definitely flunked at carrying out my responsibility. I was required to take charge, which meant that I would have to dress the corpse in her Red Cross uniform. I tried. I went into the little tent with her skirt and jacket in my arms but when I came to her body on the cot, all I could do was drop the clothes on top of her and flee.

Feeling I needed to throw myself into some new project, after that experience, I talked Eva, now my co-supervisor, into changing the existing regime. I had the new broom feeling and she was glad to go along with me, so we set about finding an easier way of getting our donuts out over our huge territory. We got out a map, marked all the locations, reasoning that if we could establish permanent quarters for each Clubmobile, it would save wear and tear on the personnel and the Clubmobiles. We had to get the okay from all Headquarters involved, both Army and Red Cross, and to find suitable quarters to house them. This took about a month, but finally it was accomplished. Headquarters at Corps Rear was happy, for it meant they could have their mansion back, which was, after all, the best of the lot. I think that they were beginning to regret their magnanimous gesture. The girls were happy, even though it meant leaving Starnberg. They were so weary of their one-night stands that when we took them to their new quarters, they acted like brides being carried over the thresholds.

This new arrangement was fine except for one constant hurdle: getting in touch with the different quarters. We had the Army telephone all right, but it seldom worked as an instrument of communication. Day after day we went through the same process, taking up the receiver with prayer and hope. Corps Rear would answer and, because they knew who we were, they would ring Army in Munich without any shenanigans. But from then on, it was hours of trying to get from one place to another with the same rigmarole. You had to go through the different stations like "Yellow Dog", "Purple Cat" to get to Company Abel, for example, with five minutes of repartee in between, when they heard our American female voices. And in the end more often than not we found only a gurgling noise at the end.

It was almost easier and quicker to drive the fifty or so miles to the different stations, so one of us often flung on a coat and flounced out the door, saying in the pidgin English of our donut makers which had become contagious. "I take jeep. I go. I be back soon."

And fly down the Autobahn, check on the girls, deliver messages and mail, get reports and be back again before the other one got through on the phone.

Almost before we had everyone settled in, Eva left for home. When the news came from HQ that you were slated on the next shipment, there was no hesitation. And shortly thereafter sometime in September Jack also got his notice that he was home-bound. We said our goodbyes with no tears. His mind was focused on going home, and he was so happy over the thought, I was happy for him. Our rapport had been a chapter to be closed with no regrets and only fond memories. It had been an instance of an isolated adventure to a different world, and now we were returning to our respective lives, so far removed from each other.

"It has been great," Jack said. "I'll never forget you. And I hope you . . . I hope you have a wonderful life. And I leave the Chevy to you, with love." He handed me the keys. "Maybe you can sell it."

"If I do I'll see that you get your half," I said, half jokingly.

Several weeks before, we had passed an abandoned, old Chevy by the side of the road several times. Jack had looked at it with great interest and, with his special aptitude, finally somehow tinkered with it until it was in good running order. How great to have an American sedan. We rode down the highway, with the feeling that the kilometers had snapped back like a rubber band.

The strange part was that I did sell it to a Russian who was desperate for a car, shortly before I was to leave for home. This Russian gave me a thousand dollars, which was still a lot of money, and I accepted quickly. Oddly enough, it seemed quite a normal transaction of its time. We had merely found an abandoned car, Jack had fixed it, given it to me and the Russian wanted it. No bill of sale, no paper work, no registration. Today, I look back with a shake of my head. And the end of the story is also a little curious. I got in touch with Jack and told him to meet me when my ship bound for New York stopped in Boston. And when the ship came into port, there he was. I handed him the half I'd promised him-five hundred dollars. He was surprised by the amount and grateful that I remembered. He gave me a thank-you kiss on the cheek and a friendly bear hug which seemed an appropriate end to our relationship.

Soon after he left, while I was still in the ETO the Army was running regular sightseeing tours all over Europe for the many furloughs and passes being handed out, and with most everyone it was a toss-up between Switzerland or the Riviera. I chose the Riviera, because by the last of October, snow was already on the ground, and the prospect of sunshine and sea was very tempting.

I left Munich one day, and a few hours later stepped out into brilliant sunshine, my Stadium boots strangely out of place. The Cote D' Azure was dazzlingly bright, and I spent a week congratulating myself on my choice. Because of my quasi-vacation from it, I found I had a renewed enthusiasm for the American uniform. The first time I went to the beach as I was putting on my bathing suit it occurred to me that without my Red Cross uniform no one would know I was an American—not an inviting thought. So, when I got there and was immediately surrounded by GI's who wanted to know where I was from, I was baffled for the first few seconds. But then I looked around. It was very easy to see that no other woman on the whole beach was as well covered in a bathing suit as I was. It was the first time I, or any of the GI's, had encountered a bikini. To be so easily distinguishable by my American one-piece suit gave me a feeling of great satisfaction.

At the end of the week, I felt the way you are supposed to feel after a vacation, but seldom do. As a group of us sat in the shade of the station waiting for our planes to take us back to our bases, I looked around at the familiar faces with renewed fondness for these guys. I could even smile indulgently at the GI who proclaimed he was going to marry the French girl he had met the night before because she was the best dancer he had ever run across.

"Why not?" I said. "At least you'll have that in common."

This restoration of enthusiasm was so thorough that I was almost disappointed when I returned to Starnberg and was told that I was slated for home. Almost disappointed, but not quite. I had a month before my two years was up but I could not help being excited at the prospect of the States and Christmas at home.

I hardly had time to say goodbye to all of Group H before I was once again in Munich, this time waiting for a train. The ride from Munich to Paris was one that left me even happier at the prospect of home and comfort. The train left in the evening, and we rode through the night with absolutely no heat and the temperature around freezing. Three nurses and I shared the double seats facing each other, and we all curled up into a ball as best we could, wishing desperately for some sort of cover. One of these nurses kept breaking into tearful diatribes against the Army for exposing her to such a cruel, cold fate. I wondered where in the world she had spent the War that she could have preserved such an attitude. The other two nurses said nothing, but I could not conceal my annoyance and finally told her off, not very politely.

"Oh, shut up," I said. "Crying isn't going to get you anyplace. Is this the worse thing you ever experienced over here? If so, you must be a real newcomer." Which just made her cry more.

Later I felt a little ashamed of myself. Nonetheless, at the same time in the back of my mind, a certain kind of sneaky pride crept in at the notion that I'd come a long way from the inhibited, homesick girl starting out on this expedition. Back then, I could never have mustered up the nerve to speak up like that.

In Paris I awaited shipment to Le Havre, and once there, I drew a Liberty Ship along with seven girls I'd never seen before and a boatload of GI's. It was quite luxurious compared to the trip over. We even had an actual stateroom. It should have been a joyous voyage, but we ran into a rough gale about the third day out, and most of the human cargo was pretty seasick. Then someone started talking about a Liberty Ship that had broken in two in just such a gale and soon everyone on the ship had visions of dying miserably and ingloriously on the way home after sweating out the War. It seemed quite credible when one felt the awful plunk every time the ship met a wave.

This pessimistic attitude gave me plenty of opportunity to exercise my cheering-up facilities, which I had honed over the previous two years. Because it had always worked well, I formed a trio with two GI's and we worked up a version of "Sentimental Journey," stepping in as the entertainment at a quickly organized get-together on deck. The seas became a little calmer and everyone brightened up visibly.

Because the sun stayed with us longer each day as we traveled west, we sat on the deck far into the night, congratulating ourselves over and over again, in one way or another, for we were the lucky ones who were on the way home. It was very comforting now, especially after the gale, to look out over the calm water as we glided safely over it on the way to that cherished destination, now almost in sight.

Sailing into the Boston Harbor that night, I was sitting with a group of GI's joking and laughing, but consumed with the thought of how glad I would be to see my family, when one of them, a great joker of obvious Italian descent, remarked in his stand-up comedic role, "Ya know what I'm gonna do when I get home? Just grab my mudder and tie myself to her apron strings. Ya betcha. Dat's for me."

We laughed heartily, since we could all empathize completely. A few minutes later someone asked our trio for that song again, and we complied with alacrity. It fitted everyone's mood and It seemed a fitting way to sing my way home: "Gonna' take a sentimental journey . . . . Sentimental journey—HOME."

EPILOGUE

T he first thing I did, after getting settled in the New York hotel which the Red Cross had arranged for us, was to call home. I gave the long distance operator our telephone number in Seattle, and my mother answered—just like that. I was completely awe struck. It seemed like a miracle to hear her voice so strong and clear after the many days of frustrating phone calls in Starnberg. I could hardly find my voice and when she heard mine, hers started to get a little shaky. She told me that my favorite great aunt had just died, which gave us license to go ahead and break down a little. When we pulled ourselves together, she told me she was coming to New York and then to a convention in Washington D. C. so I should wait and come home with her as she was leaving the next day by train and would see me in New York in five days.

I thought this would be a good opportunity to visit my good friend, Dee, who had left Starnberg three months before. She lived in York, Pennsylvania, a town I had never heard of before I met her, but on the map it seemed like a mere hop from New York, so I called her, and she invited me to visit her for a few days. She met me at the station and after we got over all the gossip on the drive home, she said, "Oh, B.J. I have just the man for you. He was engaged to my sister, and he's just like a brother to me. I've invited him over for the evening. You'll love him. His name is Norman Olewiler."

I thought to myself, "Oh, Dee. You know I don't care to see anyone but you. I've seen enough men lately." But I said, "How in the world do you spell his name?"

She spelled it for me and explained that like most people around York County, he was Pennsylvania Dutch, which was really German, It was definitely not love at first sight. When he came in the door I was not ready to be impressed, but I noted his blue eyes and dark hair which made him look more Irish than German and his thick eyebrows with hardly any arch, which gave him an earnest look. We had a big argument that evening over some forgotten premise, and we said good night rather coolly. I thought that was the end of that.

But Dee did not give up. He had promised to drive us to Baltimore the next day for her dentist's appointment, but he called that morning to renege on his promise. I heard Dee on the telephone using her feminine wiles, which she could do, urging him to come. She paid no attention to my "forget-it" signals, and he finally agreed.

On the way to Baltimore, things became interesting when he mentioned he had heard a new song that he thought was great. He said it was called "It Might As Well Be Spring," and he sang some of it for us. Dee said she thought it wasn't very melodious, but I was thrilled with it. I asked him to sing it again, and as I listened to his nice strong voice, suddenly it did seem like spring. (Of course, it was to become our song.) While Dee was in the dentist's office, he and I went to a bar on Charles Street to wait for her. I was in my Red Cross uniform, and several GI's seeing me there approached me with "Where are you from?" or some variation. I responded in the usual way, but it didn't take long to see that my new friend was a little taken aback by these exchanges. I carefully explained to him that this was not like being picked up, but as long as I had the uniform on it was to be expected.

As I did so, I was thinking, "What is this? Why should I have to explain? And why should he care, and why should I care if he cares?" I looked at him in his overcoat and hat, thinking of the contrast with a uniform. "Wait a minute," I said to myself, "you're just being carried away by the sight of a man in a civilian coat and hat."

Still, when Dee, the matchmaker, insisted that we go dancing alone that evening at a local club, because he was the best dancer in town, I didn't resist. She was right about his dancing, and I thought back to the GI who said he was going to marry the French girl because of her dancing ability. Somehow it didn't seem so foolish. We talked way into the night and I began to think that Dee was right after all; she knew we would have a lot in common. And when he kissed me good night at her front door I knew it would not be the last time.

A few days later, when I was to return to New York to meet my mother, I persuaded him to come along with me, which he was happy to do, (I learned later that he had to borrow the money for the trip, which seemed the right thing to do.) We spent three days in New York. It was a glorious experience to buy some new clothes and get out of my uniform. I was staying at the Waldorf with my mother, and I got to wear my new cocktail hat with a little feather on it that night when he came to dinner with us. We were to meet him in the lobby and I saw him first. When he recognized me, I beheld my feelings become mirrored in his eyes.

Mother went on to her conference in D. C. for three days and it seemed quite natural that I should accompany him to Carlisle where he was soon to return to law school. We spent our days walking around the town drinking dozens of cups of coffee and discussing our future. I don't think he ever proposed. It was just as if it were a tacit agreement with difficulties to be solved. The main problem was that I was supposed to go on to Japan. (In Paris on the way home, I had discovered that the Red Cross was still sending personnel to the Pacific for the Occupation. With no hesitation, I signed up when asked if I were interested in going on to Japan after one month's leave at home.) That was something I wanted to do, but we knew that if I did go on to Japan we would never see each other again. We also knew that if I called off Japan to get married, we would have known each other altogether ten days before we made this huge decision. Ten days! Sensible people don't take such chances, and we were sensible people. On the other hand—and the other hand won. I would go home to Seattle, arrange a small wedding and he would come out right after Christmas.

When I met my mother in D.C., the first thing I told her was that I was not going to Japan but was going to get married. She was overjoyed, as I expected her to be. She didn't even bring up the fact that we knew each other such a short time.

Six weeks later we were married in Seattle. As I went to meet him at the train I couldn't seem to bring his face into focus in my mind and started to worry that I might not recognize him. But as he stepped off the train, I knew I needn't have worried.

We had agreed during those long talks in Carlisle that since there were no graduate courses at Dickinson College I would have to go someplace else to continue my education, which I wanted to do, while he was going to law school. Norman had finished one year before he got drafted into the army and sent overseas. (He came down with trench foot after six weeks on the front line and was sent back to the states for possible amputation of some toes, which was avoided.) So when we came back to Carlisle and were living in the empty fraternity house before school opened, we went to Philadelphia to enroll me in the University of Pennsylvania and look for an apartment for me. We had difficulty finding one—housing was hard to come by all over the states at that time. We went back to Carlisle a little discouraged. The whole idea of living apart and seeing each other only on week ends was looking less and less inviting to both of us. That night Norman sat straight up in bed with "I have an idea. Why don't you stay here and go to law school?"

I had never entertained the idea of being a lawyer, but after some thought, I decided to give it a try. I would have a year longer to go than Norman, but the attraction of being together was very strong, so I enrolled in the law school. There was only one other woman enrolled in the whole school, and she dropped out after the first semester! I stayed for two. Every course in this school was marked with a numerical grade, so at the end of the semester you were ranked accordingly. At the end of my second semester. the only woman in a class of one hundred men, I came out ranked first; due, I am sure, to the fact that I I was five years older than most of the men and had had experience in the working world before going over seas. I knew what a chattel mortgage was.

Unfortunately, this was not the good news it might have been. Even though Norman was not in my class, he took an unmerciful beating about who would be "wearing the pants" in our house. It's hard to remember that not so long ago this phrase held the meaning it did. "To wear the pants" was to be the male in charge of all aspects of a marriage,—the way it should be.

And then, when we came to York where I had to be interviewed by a committee of the Bar Association for approval, their opening question was "Why would you ever want to be a lawyer?" From there, they made it known in no uncertain tones that I would be a hindrance rather than a help to my husband if I set myself up as an equal in his law practice. No woman had ever practiced law in this town. People were just not going to come to a woman. I know this seems hard to believe when you see the number of women lawyers vying with each other in today's world, but things really were that different just over fifty years ago.

If I had started out with a great desire to be a lawyer, I think my sense of injustice would have kept me going. As it was, when I saw so many obstacles being put in my way and I was also running out of money, I had a "sour grapes" reaction. I didn't want to be a lawyer, anyway, I decided. I could see there would be enough adjustment in married life without adding another hurdle. I must admit the dean of the law school, who was noted for never calling on a woman in one of his classes, did offer me a job in the library, but I declined. So when Norman passed the bar exams we settled in York, which I expected to be temporary, but turned out to be decidedly permanent.

Eventually, I got back to my ambition to continue my education. I had always had a great interest in Philosophy, and I met Mr. Francis Farquhar, a magnificent old man of ninety-two who had the same interest. Together we started reading the different philosophers on a weekly basis. He showed me how life can be worth living into old, old age by keeping alive the ability to wonder. I wanted to learn more, so after our daughter had reached school age, I commuted to Johns Hopkins University in Baltimore—just fifty miles away—and received my doctorate in Philosophy in my forties. I taught at the local college, York College of Pennsylvania, as an adjunct professor for sixteen years.

When Norman died in 1999, we had been married for fifty three years.